THE METAVERSE: FICTIONAL UNIVERSE

ANURAG MAURYA

Contents

Contents

Introduction

The metaverse concept was already living and fast-developing even before Facebook was renamed Meta, and CEO Mark Zuckerberg talked about "the metaverse" at length. There's no getting around it: the metaverse has here, and it's most likely here to stay. So, what exactly is the metaverse? Is it as significant as some corporations claim, or is it merely a fleeting fad that will fade away in a few months? Do you need to know everything there is to know about the metaverse, and should you get engaged before it explodes anymore? This book goes into the metaverse concept, discussing its past, present, and, most importantly, future.

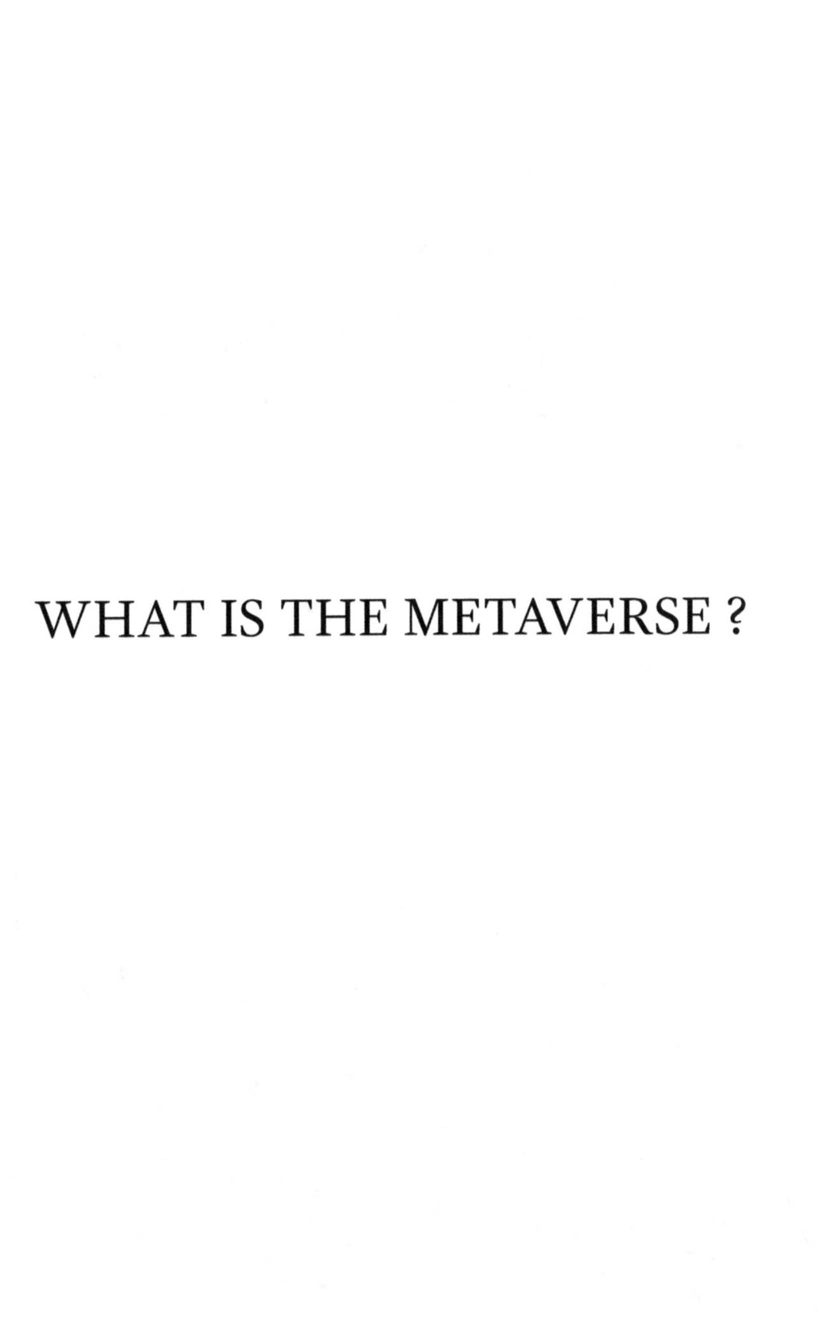

WHAT IS THE METAVERSE ?

METAVERSE EXPLAINED — EVERYTHING YOU NEED TO KNOW

Imagine a virtual world where people live, work, shop and interact with others - all from a comfortable couch in the real world.

This is what we call the metaverse.

It wasn't until Facebook changed its name to Meta in October 2021 that metaverse became a household word. In order to realize its vision for the metaverse, the company announced its plan of spending $10 billion on technology development in the year 2022.

The metaverse is considered to be the next evolutionary stage of the Internet. It will take in multiple forms including games, online communities and business meetings, allowing people to collaborate through digital avatars of themselves.

What is the Metaverse ?

Metaverse is a new beginning to create something new, much like the early days of the Internet. Billions are being invested in building metaverse, and tech tycoons call it the future, but what is metaverse? THE TERM "METAVERSE" WAS COINED BY AUTHOR Neal Stephenson in his 1992 novel Snow Crash.. Its most basic definition refers to "the concept of a fully immersive virtual world where we can work, play, relax, transact and socialize." It is a simulated digital environment that combines augmented reality (AR), virtual reality (VR), blockchain, and social media principles to create areas for rich user interaction that imitate the real world.

The concept of metaverse is not new. It first appeared in the 1992 novel "Snow Crash". Several companies have since developed online communities based on this concept, most notably Second Life, which was released in 2003.

In virtual worlds, people use avatars that represent themselves to communicate with each other and build communities virtually. In this world, digital currency is used to buy clothes, weapons and shields in video games and many other items. Users can also use virtual reality headsets and controllers to traverse the virtual world for fun without any concrete consideration.

"Snow Crash" portrays a dystopian view of the future which doesn't represent a positive view of the metaverse. The term Metaverse, coined by the author Neal Stephenson, refers to the next generation of virtual reality-based Internet. One way to gain status in Stephenson's virtual world is through technical skills, which manifest themselves in the complexity of the user's digital incarnation. Another metric is the ability to access certain restricted environments, the precursor to the registration requirements that some websites are using today.

Ready Player One is another novel by Ernest Cline that helped popularize the concept of the metaverse, and was later made into a movie directed by Steven Spielberg. This 2011 dystopian science fiction, set in 2045, describes how people escape the problems plaguing the earth by entering a virtual world called Oasis. Users access the world using a virtual reality mask and haptic gloves that allow them to grasp and touch objects in a digital environment.

How is the metaverse different from the Internet?

The Internet is a network of billions of computers, servers and other electronic devices. Once online, Internet users can communicate with each other, browse and interact with websites, as well as buy and sell goods and services.

The Metaverse does not compete with the Internet; it is built on top of it. In the Metaverse, users use technologies such as virtual reality (VR), augmented reality (AR), artificial intelligence, social media and digital currency in the virtual world that simulates aspects of the physical world. The Internet is where people browse things. But, to some extent, people can live in a virtual world. Even governments may extend their influence into the virtual world. For example, while most countries/regions have a relatively fixed presence on the Internet, Barbados opens its diplomatic embassies in the virtual world, especially in an online world called Decentraland.

The growth of the Internet has given rise to numerous services that lead the way in the creation of the metaverse. Ben Bajarin, an analyst at Creative Strategies comments, "you have a digital self on social media." Now he says it's a question of what form the metaverse will eventually take. Will it be as open as the Internet, or will it be more like a closed experience controlled by a few big companies? "The giants all want to be first pioneers and create an ecosystem of their own," Bagarin said.

Companies of Metaverse

Let's look at some examples of companies that are constructing their worlds of metaverse.

Facebook

Facebook CEO Mark Zuckerberg says his company's investment in the metaverse represents a fundamental change: that Facebook is more a company of metaverse rather than a company of Facebook. This is an important change as it means that users eventually won't need a Facebook account to use other services in the Metaverse. In fact, Facebook has already sold millions of Oculus VR headsets for navigating through virtual worlds.

Epic Games

Epic Games has a different vision for the metaverse than Facebook's in that it wants to provide a public space for interactions between users and brands, rather than a news feed filled with ads. "I strongly believe this is in line with our goal of making the world an emotional place through the power of creativity and technology," said Kenichiro Yoshida, chairman, president and chief executive officer of Sony Group Inc. in a statement.

Microsoft

Microsoft released Mesh for Microsoft Teams this year, a counterpart to the software giant's online meeting competitor Zoom. This is the latest service that allows its users in different physical locations to join in a holographic experience of collaboration and sharing during virtual meetings.

Microsoft describes Mesh as a platform that allows users to create virtual presences on any device with their own customized avatars, including a set of AI tools, session management, spatial rendering, multi-user synchronization, and holographic transfer. Holoportation is a 3D motion capturing technology that allows users to reconstruct and deliver high-quality, real-time 3D models.

Microsoft has partnered with Accenture, a professional services company, to create Mesh-enabled immersive spaces. There are more than 100,000 new employees in Accenture each year and Mesh is adopted to help them onboard. New hires meet on Teams to receive instructions on how to create a digital presence and access One Accenture Park — a shared virtual space that is part of the onboarding process. The future park-style amusement space includes a central meeting room, a virtual conference room and a digital monorail for new hires to visit different exhibits.

How does NFT integrate into the Metaverse?

Non-fungible tokens (i.e. NFTs) play an important role in the utility and popularity of the metaverse. As a secure type of digital assets, NFT is based on the same blockchain technology used by cryptocurrencies. An NFT can represent an artwork, a song, or digital real estate rather than a currency. It provides the owner with a digital protocol or proof of ownership that can be bought and sold in the metaverse.

Metaverse Properties, which claimed itself to be the world's first virtual real estate company, acts as an agent to facilitate the purchase or lease of property or land in several virtual spaces, including Decentraland, Sandbox, Somnium and Upland. Their products include meeting/commercial spaces, art galleries, family homes and gathering places.

While the Metaverse offers new companies like Metaverse Properties the opportunity for digital goods, established brick-and-mortars are also getting on board. For example, Nike acquired RTFKT, a company that produces one-of-a-kind virtual sneakers and digital artifacts with NFT, blockchain authentication and augmented reality. Prior to the acquisition, Nike filed seven trademark applications to help create and market virtual sneakers and apparel. Nike also partnered with Roblox in developing Nikeland, a digital world where Nike fans can play games and dress their avatars with virtual clothing.

"NFT and blockchain lay the foundation for digital ownership," said Nick Donarski, CEO of ORE System, an online community of gamers, content creators and game developers. "The ownership of one's real-world identity will be extended into the virtual world, and NFT will be the tool for that."

How far away is the metaverse?

While the basic idea of participating in the virtual online world has been around for years, it will still take years before it is truly capable of realistic interaction. Co-founder of Microsoft Bill Gates noted that most people don't have VR goggles and motion-capture gloves to accurately capture their expressions, body language and voice quality. But for businesses, Gates predicts that within the next two to three years, most virtual meetings will be transferred from a 2D square box to a metaverse, that is, a 3D space where participants appear as digital avatars.

CHAPTER TWO

METAVERSE: FUTURE OF THE INTERNET

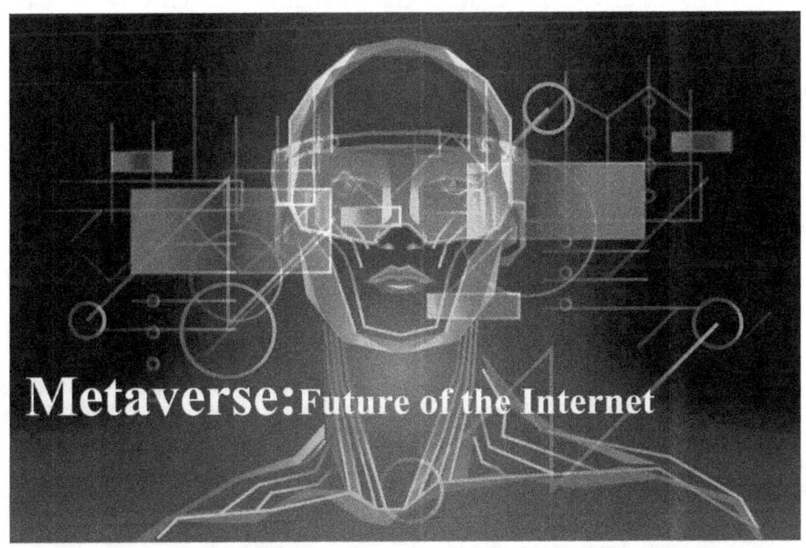

Background

The story that can now be coined as the turn of the Internet development happened on October 29, 2021, when Mark

Zuckerberg, founder of Facebook, announced that the parent company of Facebook, Whatsapp and Instagram would change its name from 'Facebook' to 'Meta'. Upon his announcement, although the names and technologies of its apps remained the same—Facebook remained Facebook, and Instagram Instagram—the Internet went frenzy.

This suggests the determination of the company, as Mark made it known in explaining its plans for the futuristic Meta project, which would enable users to connect with their family, co-workers, friends, and colleagues, on a deeper level.

He claimed, "Our overarching goal across all of these initiatives is to help bring the metaverse to life." And that is why he introduced the metaverse, where users would have their digital avatars that can be present at any given time in the virtual space. This avatar can attend meetings, have a date and even hang out with friends far away in other countries.

Defining the Metaverse

Before Mark Zuckerberg announced the name changing of Facebook at Connect 21, Metaverse was no more than a concept for a long time. "The metaverse is a massively scaled and interoperable network of real-time rendered 3D virtual words which can be experienced synchronously and persistently by an effectively unlimited number of users with an individual sense of presence and with continuity of data, such as identity, history, entitlements, objects, communications, and payments", wrote the Venture capitalist Mathew Ball.

Combining all the points of view above, it is clear that to bring forth the realization of the metaverse, it's inevitable to merge various elements of technology which will enable users to have a close to real-life experience in a digital space.

Further Comprehension

Just recall the time when you played a video game with a virtual reality (VR) experience, that is, playing a game with your VR headset on, and everything feels so real like you are actually in the game. You find yourself chased by a monster in the digital world, as you running and screaming. At that moment, you have completely gotten lost in a video game. Once you remove the VR headset, you are back to life. And think of GTA San Andreas. There are NPCs in the video game, who you could shoot at, kill for free and get away with it. Their actions and reactions are programmed, and are just there for fun of it. That is why you find it easy playing a particular video game at a certain level, as nothing has changed in the same level with same characters. The only difference is how you choose to play the game. And the metaverse is no difference from that. It is simply virtual or augmented reality in a broader sense. The major exception is that there is no NPC out there in the metaverse; there are only people like yourself, who are as real as you. They wouldn't be restricted to programmed actions and reactions like in video games. Everything happens in the metaverse are just the way it will happen in real life, only in a digital space.

When will the metaverse come true?

Mark Zuckerberg predicted that it might take 5-10 years until the metaverse go mainstream. Some elements of it are enjoyed by us now, as ultra-fast broadband speeds, virtual reality headsets, and persistent always-on online worlds are keys to which many people now have access. Tech giants are hence investing in huge volumes to develop their digital assets for the mainstream anticipation. Microsoft, Meta, Roblox, Epic Games, Minecraft, Sandbox, to mention but a few are racing towards this direction. It seems obvious that metaverse is a gateway to a new level of digital economy for both users and creators in the future.

CHAPTER THREE

Who Is Building the Metaverse? More than 150 Companies

The Internet is now a ubiquitous technology. Only 7% of Americans say they do not use the Internet, while 90% consider it essential during the Covid pandemic. In the UK, an even higher

94.8% of the population relies on Internet connectivity. So when a company commits to building the next iteration, either the physical Internet or metaverse, it is sure to raise some important questions.

How will this new Internet experience, known as the metaverse, change our lives? Will it affect businesses and the way we work? And, most importantly, who is building this new Internet that will connect more than 1 billion users by 2031? The answers to these questions are interesting and multifaceted.

What does it mean to build the metaverse?

The metaverse is defined as a unified 3D virtual world in which users can aggregate and perform complex interactions through their digital selves (i.e., avatars). The metaverse was originally conceived by science fiction author Neal Stephenson as a metaphor for the real world, an embodiment of the Internet, and an escape from reality. The concept shot to fame after Facebook's mid-year earnings call in 2021, when it announced a massive investment in building the metaverse. Soon after, it changed its name to Meta, and almost simultaneously, technology giants like Epic Games, Microsoft, and Niantic decided to pour millions of dollars into the technology.

But what does it really mean to build a metaverse? Unlike most virtual reality applications, the metaverse is not a single software platform that can be built using the usual agile development models. Instead, it is a complex digital environment that relies on seven different layers

Building the Metaverse

1. **Infrastructure : 5G, Wi-Fi, cloud and other connectivity technologies and high-tech materials such as GPUs**

2. **Human-Machine Interface: Users will join virtual worlds using VR headsets, AR glasses, haptics and other technologies**

3. Decentralization: Blockchain, artificial intelligence, edge computing and other democratization tools

4. Spatial computing: 3D visualization and modeling frameworks

5. Creator economies: a variety of design tools, digital assets and e-commerce institutions

6. Discovery: Content engines that drive engagement, including advertising, social media, ratings, reviews, etc.

7. Experience: VR equivalents of digital apps for gaming, events, work, shopping, etc.

Here's the interesting part: there are currently more than 160 companies operating in these seven vertical areas, and together they are building the metaverse.

Now Top Companies building the metaverse

When Facebook changed its name to Meta, the industry was eager to realign its investments and support anyone who could build the future. But the question is, who is building the metaverse? How do you determine ownership of what is essentially a decentralized and democratized concept? As Meta makes clear in its statement, no company will own the Metaverse. Multiple organizations, independent developers and grassroots creators — and the final piece of the puzzle we'll discuss later — will build the metaverse. Several companies have already started investing in this direction.

Facebook (Meta)

Facebook owns most of the seven infrastructure elements we discussed for building the metaverse. Thanks to its line of Oculus headsets, its massive social media advertising engine, and its burgeoning creator economy, it can successfully launch working prototypes within 2 to 5 years.

Microsoft

At the same time, Microsoft is looking to build a work-centric metaverse that will connect its popular products into a digital environment called Mesh. In Mesh, you'll be able to use Microsoft Teams, Windows and other services in VR.

Decentraland

Decentraland is one of the first movers to explicitly make the metaverse its core product. Since its inception in 2017, Decentraland has grown steadily - a piece of real estate in its VR world recently sold for a record $2.4 million.

Apple

Apple may be a surprising dark horse in the virtual world race. It is currently working on advanced VR devices that could revolutionize the virtual world experience. Morgan Stanley even says that mass market adoption of the metaverse depends on Apple, just as the smartphone and tablet markets did before it.

Nividia

While Nvidia is not directly building its own metaverse, it will be a key enabler. 2021 sees its release of Omniverse Enterprise, in which creators can collaborate on 3D modeling, design and simulation. Omniverse lays the foundation for the metaverse by combining 3D graphics with AI and supercomputing.

Epic Games

This company behind the popular immersive game Fortnite is always perfectly poised to build virtual worlds. It formalized its intentions this year with the announcement of a $1 billion funding round to drive growth opportunities in the metaverse.

Niantic

Niantic's Pokémon Go is one of the first immersive experiences to blur the line between the real and the virtual. Now, the company has raised $300 million to build its own virtual worlds, which will replace the original notion of virtual worlds as dystopian nightmares.

Can the construction of a metaverse be attributed to a specific territory?

This is an important question because some experts believe that the metaverse can operate as a separate region, almost like a nation-state, with its own economy and population.

While most of the companies we are discussing are located in the US, EU and UK, China is also taking action. China is steadily gaining ground in building complex artificial intelligence, and most virtual reality manufacturing is happening in China. It remains to be seen whether Chinese tech giants like Tencent will act on their currently fledgling plans to build virtual worlds.

The central piece of the metaverse puzzle is you

This early flurry of activity led to a unique conclusion: the secret to building a successful metaverse is user adoption and ultimately user-generated content. the rapid rise of Facebook was closely tied to the growth in the number of users, as was the case with Microsoft, Decentraland, and others. This is probably the biggest hurdle. Some 30 years have passed since the birth of the Internet, and we have yet to achieve 100% Web 2.0 penetration. As the metaverse is built, stakeholders must focus on minimizing adoption barriers and addressing user hesitations to make it successful.

CHAPTER FOUR

METAVERSE: USE CASES AND CONCERNS

As we concluded previously, metaverse is the next internet. Before going into analyzing some typical use cases in the industry, we should be aware that, with a fast growing speed, metaverse is becoming a trillion-dollar worth industry. For anything at such scale, effective rules and regulations, standards and practices are urgently asked for, and that is the most concerning part of the metaverse.

Use-cases in The Metaverse

As we live in the world of the Internet, we are already in some way in part of the metaverse. The apps on our phones are getting ready for connection to the world. As the internet becomes more and more expansive, it will eventually develop into the metaverse. Let's take a closer look at some use cases here:

1. Flexible Working Locations

More and more tools and technology are now setting the work environment free from location and businesses. The pandemic Covid-19 could be the turning point in the scenario as businesses were forced to adopt other forms, such as working from home, hybrid or work from anywhere, rather than what they used to. With metaverse, the transition would be smoother for both enterprises and consumers. For Microsoft Mesh and Meta's Horizon World, working from the metaverse has already become common.

2 . Marketplaces and Assets

One of the key features of the metaverse is being self-sustainable, which means a new economy that funds creators and co-creators in its own way. Co-creation is not uncommon in social media markets, such as YouTube, Snap AR Lens, Stories and Insta Reels. But in the metaverse, the funding process is claimed to be transparent with the adoption of NFT (i.e. non-fungible tokens). Numbers of marketplaces of this type are booming, e.g. Cryptopunks, Hashmasks, SuperRare, Sandbox, Rarible, NFTically and more. One typical use case for NFT includes that all confidentials/copyright assets can be made open on the marketplace, and users can use directly the original assets with the originator's permission. In this way, metaverse is not only beneficial to the creators, but also convenient for users when accessing digital content.

3. Skilling & Re-skilling

The shortage in skilled workforce has always been a predicament for industries. According to the Global Talent Crunch report, in less than 20 years time, most of the baby-boomer generation would meet their retirement age, the process of which has been made faster by Covid-19. Meanwhile, 75% of the global workforce will be millennials by 2023. For the younger generation, traditional ways of skill training are outdated and incapable of meeting the needs of enterprise complexity nowadays. Co-working with machines and on top of all, workforce safety compliance requirements are becoming trendy in industries.

In the metaverse, remote collaboration can be carried out to solve some of the challenges when it comes to workforce training and onboarding, with improvement and efficiency. Vice versa, it would make the future work and workforce more metaverse ready. With the AI empowered metaverse, needs and requirements can easily be decided, so is the remote working and controlling of machines. Better and faster decisions at work will be made, so are more effective corrections and improvements.

4. Real Estate & Event Management

Being a self-sustainable marketplace means that everything in the physical world can have a digital version in the metaverse marketplace. Niantic is now building a 3D map to augment the physical world. In the same way, viral properties can also be traded, such as house building and selling/renting, or advertisement earning on it.

Another use case is the management and organization of events and concerts. There are a lot of VR events already happening around the world, from convocation, virtual conferences to concerts and award shows. Relevant advertisement in the metaverse also provides a great opportunity, as it makes everything cost-free and open to everyone who joins in, and even gets people paid just for joining the events.

The Concerning Parts

Metaverse, like every other technological evolution ever, raises a lot of concerns as it exposes more of us and our information to the world.

1. Protecting Your Identity

Without strong laws and regulations, impersonating others is not difficult at this stage. Thus, safeguarding your future identity in the metaverse is at risk. Consider the following situations:

- What if someone accesses your assets without your knowledge?
- It is difficult to differentiate the real from the fake.
- There could be irreversible impact or social reputation caused by social media/metaverse trials.
- ......

We urgently need attention from governments, institutions, enterprises and legal authorities to make universal virtual identity possible and safe. On top of that, a common consensus among users is called for.

2. Protecting Privacy

Another major concern in the metaverse is the privacy of personal information, as we are more and more exposed and vulnerable to exploits. With surveillance cameras and smart glasses roaming and watching everywhere, we will be almost transparent.

New types of restrictions will be accordingly imposed to detect camera devices or illegitimate use of glasses in certain areas. The difficult part would be how to define the compromised privacy and how it fits in the justice system in the physical world.

3. Law and Order

Metaverse is now going through a phase without effective rules and regulations like that in the real world. Crimes like killing, cheating and posing weapons can not yet be held accountable in the metaverse. Here are concerns about dealing with them in a similar legal system.

- Will there be a metaverse constitution?

- What would the punishment be? Is a virtual jail possible?
- Will there be virtual police who can maintain law and order?
- Are there tools and technology to identify crimes in the metaverse?
- Will there be a metaverse court?

Seven Fundamental Features to Achieve The Metaverse

There has been a lot of discussion about the metaverse since its creation in the 1990s, but the buzz has evidently increased during the pandemic period, especially since Facebook changed its name to Meta. But is it an obscure marketing phrase? How do you define a metaverse? Where is the line between one metaverse and another? Let's start with an overview of how to look at the metaverse and where it intersects with the Web 3.

In many ways, the metaverse is just another name for the development of the Internet: a network that is much more social, immersive, and economically complex than it is today. In a broad sense, there are two competing visions of how to achieve this: one is all too familiar to many today - centralized, closed, and beholden to large corporations that do as they please and often extract economic revenues from its creators, contributors, and users. The other vision is decentralized, with substantial property rights and new boundaries, interoperable, open, and owned by the community that built and maintains it.

An open metaverse is decentralized, allowing users to control their own identities, enforce property rights, align incentives and ensure that users, not the platform, receive value. An open metaverse is also transparent, license-free, interoperable, and convergent.

There are seven essential features to achieve a true metaverse - whether open or closed. We believe that these are necessary to meet the minimum requirements for what is called a metaverse. Our goal is to clear out the misinformation about the metaverse for builders and potential participants, and to provide a framework for assessing the early metaverse.

1. Decentralization

Decentralization is a major concept at the origin and also an overarching governing principle that applies to the metaverse. Decentralization means not being owned or operated by a single entity nor being at the mercy of a few power brokers. A centralized platform often start out friendly and cooperative to attract users and developers, but once it slows down, competition, extraction and zeroing follow suit. Powerful intermediaries tend to abuse user rights and perform de-platforming to achieve a monopoly economy with high rates of return. With decentralized systems, more equitable ownership among stakeholders, reduce censorship, and increase diversity are made possible.

Decentralization is important, for centralized platforms cannot make the same strong commitments controlled by codes as blockchains, where commitments can be revoked or changed once an arrangement no longer makes sense. Decentralization that ensures the controlling rights is the most effective way to prevent abusive behavior and secure the metaverse world.

2. Openness/Open source

Open source is the practice of making free code available and able to be redistributed and modified at will. Open source as a principle is so important to the development of the metaverse that it makes true composability possible.

So what does open source mean in a metaverse development environment? Open source and openness help ensure that innovation happens. When code bases, algorithms, markets and protocols become transparent public products, builders can pursue their visions and ambitions by building more complex and reliable experiences.

Openness leads to more secure software and eliminates information asymmetry. These attributes can create fairer and more equitable systems that truly harmonize network participants. They can even eliminate the need for outdated U.S. securities laws, which were designed decades ago to reconcile long-standing principal-agent problems and information asymmetries in the business.

3. Community Ownership

In the metaverse, all stakeholders should have a say in the governance of the system based on their level of involvement. People should not solely follow the instructions given by a group of product managers from a technology company. The potential of a virtual world would never be reached if it is owned by any entity.

Community ownership is one piece of the puzzle that enables network participants, including builders, creators, investors and users, to collaborate with each other and work for the common good. This miracle of coordination is carefully orchestrated through the ownership of the network's native asset tokens, a collaboration that previously would not have been possible without the advent of cryptocurrencies and blockchains.

In addition to the technological advances brought by decentralization, the philosophical implications of community ownership are critical to the success of the metaverse. In Web 3, participants in decentralized autonomous organizations or DAOs have taken this principle to heart. They are shunning the formal rigidity of corporate structures in favor of more flexible and diverse experiments in democratic and informal governance. This allows communities to be managed, built and driven by users rather than by entities.

4. Immersive socialization

Large technology companies try to make you believe that high-performance virtual reality or augmented reality (VR/AR) hardware is essential, perhaps even the most important, part of realizing the metaverse. Companies see these hardware as the primary computing interface providers for 3D virtual worlds, but they are also bottlenecks for people to experience across borders.

The existence of the metaverse is maintained by social immersion in a broad sense. The types of activities enabled by the metaverse are more important than hardware like VR/AR. They will allow people to hang out remotely, work together, connect with friends and have fun, just as they do today with Discord, Twitter Spaces or Clubhouse.

The surge in the use of other teleconferencing and telepresence tools (e.g., Zoom) during the Covid pandemic underscores the need for a more immersive experience that goes beyond traditional text-based communication platforms like email. Moreover, because of the economic elements outlined earlier in the article, namely, property rights, self-sovereignty and community ownership, the metaverse allows people to earn a living, get engaged in commerce, and gain social status. In the typical knowledge worker workplace, people use tools like Slack to collaborate, while outside the traditional corporate world, Discord and Telegram are prevalent in the bottom-up organizing movement of DAO.

The metaverse has nothing to do with the "view" mode, the tool that is used to view the metaverse. For those who control the manufacturing hardware, it is just a way to facilitate the meme.

5. Composability

Composability is a principle of system design, specifically the ability to mix and match software components. Each software component needs to be written only once and can be reused afterwards. In order to be composable, the metaverse must provide high quality, open technical standards. In games such as Minecraft and Roblox, users can create digital goods and new experiences with the basic components provided by the system, but it is difficult to move them out of that environment or modify its inner workings. Companies that provide embedded services, such as Stripe for payments or Twilio for communications, can work across websites and applications, but they don't allow external developers to change their black-box code.

In its most powerful form, composability and interoperability are possible across a wide range of software stacks. Decentralized finance or DeFi is a typical example. Anyone can tweak, recycle, change or import existing code. Developers can also build real-time programs, such as Compound's lending protocols or Uniswap's automated market-making (AMM) transactions, in the memory of a shared virtual computer (i.e. Ethereum). By combining new elements of property rights, identity and ownership, builders can create entirely new experiences.

6. Self-sovereignty

Identity is closely related to property rights. As in the real world, you can't own anything if you can't own yourself. People should not be completely dependent on a small group of centralized identity providers for their identities; their identities must be able to persist throughout the metaverse.

Authentication is about identity, specifically, proving who the person is, what they have access to and what information they share. The largest tech platforms on the web today, such as Meta and Google, use social sign-in or single sign-on (SSO) to collect data to monitor people's behavior and provide models for developing more relevant advertisement models. In addition, with full control, the companies behind the platforms get to decide the authentication process with or without honesty and willingness.

The cryptography at the heart of Web 3 enables people to authenticate themselves, and further control their own identity themselves or with the help of a service of their choice. Wallets (e.g. Metamask and Phantom) provide ways for people to authenticate themselves. EIP-4361 (Ethernet Login) and ENS (Ethernet Domain Name Service) allow projects to coordinate around open source protocols and contribute independently to a richer and more secure concept of digital identity.

7. Property Rights

Today, most successful video games make money by selling in-game items, such as skins, emotes and other digital goods. But currently players actually are paying to rent them. Once a game unilaterally decides to shut down or change its rules, players would lose access to it.

This form of renting is so common in Web 2's centralized services, it makes having an actual ownership sounds so strange. But this should be a shared logic in the digital world as in the physical: when you buy something, you own it. Before cryptography, blockchain technology, and related innovations like NFT were realized, true digital property rights were not possible. As a result, the metaverse has changed the relationship between people and digital assets.

CHAPTER SIX

Metaverse Jobs in The Near Future

Metaverse Jobs in The Near Future

The metaverse could be a reality sooner than later, thanks to the efforts of various companies that are competing to be the leaders of the new "universe." The metaverse will be a fully immersive digital world for all of us, and promises to deliver exciting possibilities.

With Facebook going all in to make the metaverse a reality, and many other top tech companies joining the space, it is safe to assume the race to the metaverse is on. With new technology comes new opportunities. This piece will explore a few jobs that are likely to arise from the coming of the metaverse.

1 . Metaverse Research Scientist

Research scientists in AR and VR are already a staple of top universities and major tech companies. As metaverse becomes a widely accepted idea, you can expect to see more ads for such individuals within the space. Some experts believe that the role of these scientists will be to build something akin to the "theory of everything", wherein the entire world is visible and actionable digitally, like in the Ready Player One movie. This architecture will be the foundation upon which all other use cases will be built; games, adverts, quality control in factories, connected health, DeFi apps, etc. It is an insanely complex undertaking where candidates will need to build and then scale prototypes using technology at the confluence of computer vision algorithms in 3D.

2. Metaverse Stylist

People will exist on the metaverse using avatars that reflect themselves to some extent. With so many metaverse companies creating custom avatars and AR clothing, a metaverse stylist is likely to be a very in-demand job.

3. Metaverse Safety Manager

The internet, as it exists today, is not quite safe, and anyone that thinks that metaverse will be any different might be kidding themselves. Safety managers will have to provide guidance and oversight regarding privacy, in-world ID verification, safe headgear, adequate sensors etc. Their input will be required during design, validation, mass production stages, ensuring our digital world is safe and meets or exceeds applicable regulatory safety requirements etc., all without sacrificing cutting-edge functionality or design or cutting into revenues.

4. Metaverse Lawyer

The recent NFT boom has opened the door for digital artists, creators, musicians, athletes etc. The boom has also accelerated another industry - metaverse law. With so much movement happening in the metaverse and with alternative asset classes, it is clear the legal landscape needs to adapt just as fast.

5. Metaverse Marketer

The role of the metaverse marketer will be to launch complex and creative advertising campaigns that blur the lines between the physical and digital worlds. Just like the recently created "Chief Meme Officer" role that requires someone who has their pulse on the fast-moving internet culture and can strategize with a company on how to best connect their brand with their audience, the role of the metaverse marketer will be similar but within a new universe. To build a brand, you will likely need to purchase billboard space in a virtual world, engage with fans on a platform such as Discord, or even collaborate with Jadu or The Fabricant to create virtual assets.

6. Metaverse Tour Guide

Given that there will be an endless number of possible worlds to explore, you will probably have to rely on a metaverse tour guide to ensure you do not miss out on anything. The tour guide will jump you from one environment to another, and offer you insider knowledge on the rich history of the platform you are in, all with the goal of helping you unlock exclusive experiences.

7. Metaverse Asset Adviser

With the explosion of NFTs, a metaverse asset advisor will likely be one of the most sought-after jobs. Just like financial advisors today, these individuals will offer advice on which assets one can put their money in on the metaverse.

8. Metaverse Planner

Ideas may come to us cheaply, but executing them is expensive. Once there is a working metaverse, the ability to plan and implement all manner of functionalities into a fully virtual world will be essential for most companies. This is where the metaverse planner will come in. As company leaders set a vision and strategy for creating and growing their metaverses, the planner will need to drive a strategic portfolio of opportunities, from proof-of-concept to pilot to deployment. To achieve these goals, the planner will have to identify market opportunities, build business cases, influence engineering roadmaps, develop key metrics, etc.

CHAPTER SEVEN

METAPHYSICS... WITH THE HELP OF THE BLOCKCHAIN

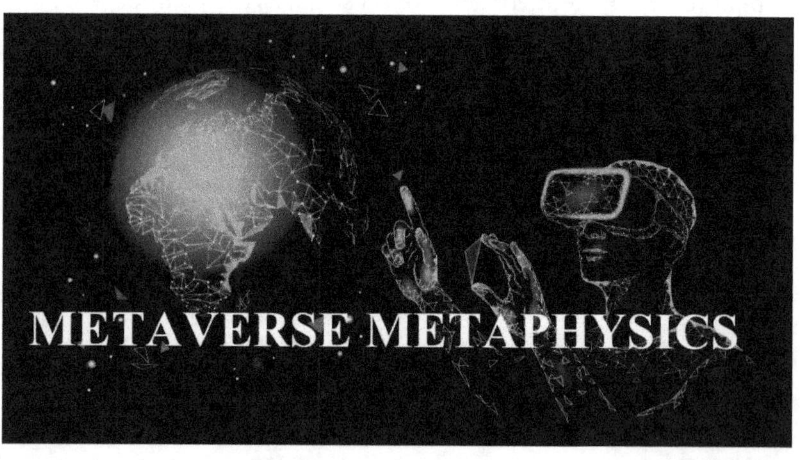

Of course, there is no underlying need for a decentralized structure, but it fits what many advocates of the Metaverse believe to be the ideal goal: Sweeney describes it as an "Open framework in which each individual can control his or her own existence without constraints.".

To create a true Metaverse, rather than a separate collection of 3D spaces, the platform needs to be interoperable and seamless. Payments must be secure, frictionless and immediate. Wherever you are in the Metaverse, you must be able to retain and use the created assets (such as your custom avatars) . Until recently, to participate in the Digital World, you had to leave a trail of bread crumbs for the gatekeeper to recognize you. When individuals use blockchains to track their accounts, assets, and transactions, it adds tremendous potential for users to choose what they can do, what they own, and what they decide to trade.

The blockchain is one of the "Central drivers" of the Metaverse, according to Matthew Ball, a venture capitalist and influential meta-commentator. He defines another key element of the Metaverse as "The individual's sense of existence and... the continuity of data". The longer you live online, the more important your personal skin becomes. Even the most basic pixel art is tied to personal identity, and as people's enthusiasm for CryptoPunks shows, its owners often say they feel connected to their punk.

In fact, NFT makes people more likely to express their personalities online, whether through randomly generated or carefully designed features. The virtual clothing and accessories that users choose in the virtual world will help everyone feel real about their online identity and deepen their participation. Fashion and art are an important part of self-expression in the real world. Why should the Online World Be Different?

As mentioned earlier, digital fashion is booming, with new growing opportunities in NFT. Design firms and celebrities are selling skin, clothes, hair and pets as NFT. "Releasing NFT" is as hot as releasing an unexpected album. Indeed, both musicians and athletes are embracing the possibility of earning royalties from the sale of NFT assets in the hope of creating a new system of property rights free of traditional broker practices.

As digital property rights become legal and blockchains become more secure, NFT could become a more important bargaining chip.

For example, imagine a team negotiating with Disney to use his role. Sound far-fetched? Sotheby's recently saw a DAO (including 17,000 donors) push the bidding for a rare copy of the US Constitution to more than $43m. Although they did not win the copy this time, it is clear that the shared ownership promoted by NFT will become a real economic force.

To fund the future

What do all these mean for capitalism, innovation and creativity? What do they mean for the business model and our life experience?

From games to tickets, from software subscriptions to health care, the Metaverse offers a range of revenue sources that could change the technological paradigm away from advertising and big data, and all the privacy and security nightmares they bring. This is certainly not inevitable, but it is at least a possibility.

The more open and accessible the platform is, the more powerful the narrative becomes. Interconnected platforms attract more users. Then, seamless, interoperable payment and asset mechanisms increase the incentive to design and transact -- to recycle revenue across the system, and increase the potential for a parallel economic discipline.

Major game companies are already making their Metaverse development tools widely available with the stated goal of encouraging interoperability for wider adoption. These companies believe that an open Mateverse is the best choice for business. This is certainly the best way to create a thriving online economy -- one in which users are motivated to participate and create value that will benefit both platform developers and user creators.

This time, the technical, philosophical and economic cases may all point in the same direction: the ability to use blockchain technology, toward a distributed Metaverse in which, online citizens can finally escape the walled garden of Web 2.0 and reap the benefits of their contributions. In this exciting new world, NFT will bridge the gap between the real and the virtual. From identity to business, tangible ownership will make all the difference. It's a whole new reality.

CHAPTER EIGHT

WHAT HAPPENS WHEN YOU DIE IN THE METAVERSE?

The metaverse is the latest buzzword in technology, and it represents an alternate universe where our digital lives catch up with the physical ones in many aspects. Companies are excited by the endless possibilities that the metaverse will usher in, and with advancements in blockchain technology, people will even be able to own assets in the metaverse in a trustless manner. This will likely create a whole new economy that one can only imagine. So far, NFTs offer a glimpse of how ownership will work in the metaverse, where individuals are able to use their digital avatars to explore the virtual world, engaging in different activities such as shopping, attending conference meetings and more.In the metaverse, our digital selves in most aspects are extensions of who we are in real life. Given that the metaverse promises to augment our physical and digital lives, one can only wonder, what will happen when we die in the metaverse?

Understanding the Metaverse

The metaverse can be described as an integrated network of 3D virtual worlds that can be accessed through a virtual reality headset. Here, users navigate the metaverse using their eye movements, feedback controllers and voice commands. The metaverse is still in its early stages of development, but to get a glimpse of the technology, you can check out popular virtual reality games such as Rec Room or Horizon Worlds, where participants use avatars to interact with each other in a virtual environment.Beyond gaming, the applications for this technology are staggering. For example, musicians and entertainment labels are experimenting with hosting concerts in the metaverse. The sports industry is also getting in on the action, with clubs such as Manchester City building virtual stadiums that will allow fans to watch games and presumably purchase virtual merchandise.

However, it is important to note that while VR is considered a key ingredient of the metaverse, experiencing the metaverse is not limited to just VR technology. Anyone with a computer or smartphone can also tap into the metaverse, through applications such as Second Life or Decentraland.

What Will Happen If You Die in the Metaverse?

Given that the metaverse attempts to bridge our digital environments (online identities) while enabling more life-like experiences, you will not be just logging online as it is usually you're your social media accounts. In the metaverse, digital avatars can be controlled through ownable assets like NFTs that can be traded or transferred to another user.

Since the metaverse promises to help us create a more permanent and controllable digital version of ourselves, it is fair to say that if you die in the metaverse, you die in real life too, since you will be losing something of value. The whole idea of the metaverse is to treat your "hyperreal" self as an actual person, and not just an account owned by Twitter or Facebook.

In today's world, people agonize over the lack of retweets or likes, and they will most likely be crushed if they get banned or restricted from their favorite social media platforms. This feeling will be heightened if the metaverse successfully integrates more real-life attributes into the digital world.

That said, the early iterations of the metaverse reside in games that simulate real life. As is the case, once you die in the game, it does not mean that you stop breathing. You continue to live physically. The real issue is that once you have established your digital self, and maybe even created some wealth through the ownership of virtual parcels of land or digital art, what happens to these assets if you die in the real world?

According to HQ Han of Protocol Labs, when a person dies in the physical world, what happens to their belongings is determined by a legal process. However, in the metaverse, code is law. Therefore "we need tools to account for inheritance and recuperation of digital assets in case of death." He adds that instead of worrying about what happens when you die in the metaverse? What might be more important is the guarantee that there is something to leave behind in the first place."

The Emerging Metaverse Economy

The Emerging Metaverse Economy

The metaverse is promising to change the way that we experience the internet forever. It is an immersive virtual world that will closely resemble the world we live in. You will be able to visit shopping centers, drive across town, meet a friend in restaurants, and exchange contacts in ways that seem strikingly real. This is thanks to the rapid advances in virtual reality and 5G communications.

The metaverse might have gained some buzz over the past few months, though these universes have existed for decades in the form of multiplayer online games. However, we are now on the cusp of entering an age of immersive experience that will be hardly distinguishable from the real world. This will foster new modes of interaction for gamers and non-gamers alike.

Already, next-generation prototype metaverses such as Decentraland and Somnium Space are showcasing the beginnings of a true digital society, where individuals settle on parcels of land, interact socially, exchange goods, and assert ownership rights. An economy is needed for any society (physical or virtual) to function. In the metaverse, the economy depends on the authentication of digital properties such as homes, cars, farms, books, clothing, and furniture. To flourish, the metaverse also needs the ability for users to travel and trade freely between realms that might have different rules.

Non-fungible tokens (NFTs), which are records of digital ownership stored in the blockchain, serve as the metaverse economy's linchpin. They enable authentication of possessions, property, and even identity. Since NFTs are secured by a cryptographic key that cannot be deleted, copied, or destroyed, it enables a robust and decentralized verification method for one's virtual identity and digital possessions, which is necessary for the metaverse society to succeed and interact with other metaverse societies.

According to Eric Anziani, COO of Crypto.com, NFTs may have started on the digital art side. However, they are going to be more powerful; they will be the tools representing any digital type of assets in virtual worlds moving forward. Looking past the multi-million-dollar digital art sector, the significance of NFTs may lie in enabling the beginnings of something resembling genuine human society based on free markets (for goods, services, and ideas), independent ownership, and social contracts to flourish in the metaverse.

A Deeper Dive into Metaverse Platforms

Decentraland is one of the most popular blockchain-based metaverses. Take a stroll through the platform, and you will discover people chatting by fountains, shoppers in fashion boutiques, joggers on seaside promenades, casino croupiers inviting guests to high stakes poker, and so on. These interactions are possible thanks to virtual real estate development by people who have purchased land and built environments that happen to capture the imagination of other Decentraland "citizens."

The experience is far from hyper-realistic, and even Decentraland creators themselves admit the **"universe"** is still in its **"iron age."** However, even in these early iterations, the potential is clear. People tend to flock to exciting places on the metaverse, just like in the physical world.

A key economic concept of Decentraland and other metaverses is the adjacency of land. All metaverse parcels are contiguous to others at a fixed location within a finite geography. This creates scarcity due to the limited amount of property supply. In turn, the scarcity enables property value to rise and fall based on universal laws of supply and demand.

Thus, a framework in line with the Decentraland manifesto is creating "a social experience with an economy driven by the existing layers of land ownership and content distribution."

for metaverse property rights, you simply cannot fake it because of the way smart contracts are defined and NFTs programmed. You know you own an asset and can demonstrate ownership fully. Based on the terms and conditions of that virtual environment, you can then assert ownership rights."

The implications of this real estate revolution are being felt emphatically. Last year in June, digital property investment fund Republic Realm bought a parcel of land in Decentraland for over $900,000. The company plans to turn the land into a virtual mall known as Metajuku, modeled after the Harajuku district in Tokyo. Such activities suggest it will not be long before real estate investment trusts (REITs) begin sniffing out opportunities in the metaverse.

"Decentraland's value proposition to application developers is that they can fully capitalize on the economic interactions between their applications and users."According to the metaverse's manifesto, "to allow those economic interactions, the platform must allow three things to be traded: currency, goods, and services."

Heating Up the Metaverse Space

Ever since Mark Zuckerberg announced that Facebook was changing its name to Meta and would become a metaverse company within the next five years, every company with a semblance of a digital presence has rushed to release shareholder statements, gave talks, or tweeted about their plans for the metaverse.

Like religious prophets, these big tech luminaries are preaching about the coming of the next iteration of the internet. Tech companies and venture capitalists believe that tomorrow's cyberspace will be empyrean, transcendent, immersive, 3D and exciting. It will be a super-platform that convenes sub-platforms; social media, online video games, and ease-of-life apps all accessible through the same digital space, and sharing the same digital economy.

Today, let us go over a few companies involved in the metaverse race.

META

To leave no doubts on the plans they have for the future, the people at Facebook have decided to change the company's name to Meta. The company has single-handedly created a lot of buzz around the term 'metaverse'. Meta has spent many years building its VR and AR portfolio, and has even begun work on its own early versions of the metaverse through its Horizons and Horizons Workrooms platforms.

In the future, the company plans to incorporate its more future-facing tech, including wrist wearable neural inputs, advanced AR glasses, and smartwatches, into a metaverse it previously described as "the next era of human-computer interaction." According to a recent poll, the only thing holding the company's ambitions back is the fact that people hate Facebook/Meta with a burning passion.

MICROSOFT

Earlier last month, Microsoft announced efforts to pursue an enterprise, office-focused metaverse by integrating AR and VR from its Microsoft Mesh platform into Teams. This means Team users wearing VR headsets could one day create customizable avatars that could mimic their facial cues and be used during video calls. The company has called the integration a "gateway to the metaverse" that they have described as "a persistent digital world that is inhabited by digital twins of people, places and things."

NVIDIA

Nvidia is another company that gave a clear roadmap for its metaverse ambition last month by announcing a new platform that would be utilized to create avatars using facial tracking, speech recognition, 3D animation, and other technologies called the Omniverse Avatar. The announcement was part of Nvidia's broader "omniverse" ambitions, which is another word for the metaverse, but with greater emphasis on technologies that interact with individuals in the real, physical world.

ROBLOX

One can argue that this company has already created some form of metaverse. Now, the plan is to expand its metaverse by providing users and developers with more tools to create experiences on their own terms, with an emphasis on safety. In a recent interview, the company's CEO David Baszucki bragged that the Roblox business model predicted the rise of the metaverse 17 years ago. As of April 2020, the company had over 203 million monthly active users that are constantly engaged in a digital second life.

NIANTIC

If we consider having a real-world impact on everyday uses, no company has arguably done more to bridge the gap between the real physical world and AR experiences than Niantic, thanks to its wildly popular Pokémon Go. The company recently announced the launch of its own augmented reality development kit known as Lightship that aims to make building AR experiences easier and more accessible. The ultimate goal of Lightship is to one day create a "real world metaverse."

QUALCOMM

Unlike most companies on this list, Qualcomm is not trying to create the ultimate metaverse that will outshine the rest. The company is instead focused on providing the building blocks for new AR apps through a platform known as Qualcomm Spaces. The company is already working with various developers, and claims that its platform will offer cross-device interoperability able to support a plethora of standalone AR devices and smartphone-powered AR devices.

SAMSUNG

Samsung has become a market leader when it comes to mobile devices, and it is no surprise the company is trying to figure out its place within the metaverse. Samsung is trying to lead the charge with its new LPDDR5X DRAM for smartphones and mobile devices. Outside of smartphones, the company believes the LPDDR5X DRAM will support high-speed future-facing applications that include the metaverse and AI, and 5G.

As the metaverse shapes up, we can expect to see this list grow over the next few years.

How Brands Can Thrive in The Metaverse

The metaverse has become somewhat of a buzzword lately. According to Cathy Hackl, Chief Metaverse Officer of Future Intelligence Group, you need to first understand the evolution of the internet to understand the metaverse. Web 1.0 helped to connect information, leading to the creation of the internet. Then came Web 2.0, which connected people through social media and brought forth the sharing economy. Now, we are witnessing the evolution of Web 2.0 to Web 3.0, which aims to connect people, spaces, and assets. These people, spaces, and assets can be in a fully virtual environment, but also be in our real world with some level of augmentation, such as through a wearable device.

These evolutions have been beneficial for various businesses; Web 3.0 is enabling the creation of the metaverse, which is a convergence of the physical and digital worlds. "Think of it as the successor of what comes next on the internet. It's like your digital lifestyle catching up to your physical life."

Blockchain Projects Represent a Small Piece of The Pie

Most individuals, especially those within crypto, may be aware of the metaverse through blockchain projects such as Decentraland.

However, according to Hackl, even mainstream companies like Snapchat are involved with the metaverse to some degree. Her view of the metaverse is quite expansive, having worked in VR hardware, spatial computing, and augmented reality hardware. Despite the buzz around blockchain metaverse projects, they represent a small slice of the overall metaverse pie, though it is increasing according to Hackl. Currently, you have SoftBank leading the investment for $93 million in Series B for the Sandbox. Meanwhile, Upland just raised $18 million with a $300 million valuation. At the same time, plenty of NFT gaming metaverses are growing at a rapid rate.

Blockchain plays a crucial role since we cannot enable an open, decentralized metaverse without it. Therefore, it is an underlying component that most of us require. This makes NFTs a bit of a stepping stone into the metaverse regarding ownership of digital assets and digital identity. "How do you actually enable that? NFTs are a big part of that equation."

The Biggest Potential for Brands

Hackl adds that she has been exploring the idea that"direct-to-avatar" might be the next "direct-to-consumer."

a stepping-stone. We use emojis when we text people; we don't even write anymore. We use an emoji to represent a message. Our emojis – and by extension, our avatars – are becoming emotional surrogates of ourselves."

Representing yourself as an avatar is a big thing because it is a moment of self-expression. The question now is, how do brands play into that? People will want to outfit their avatars, maybe through fashion brands like Adidas.

Another good example is what Samsung Bitmoji enables one to do with their avatars or Snapchat. In such a scenario, people will be concerned with how their avatar shows up, how it will look like, how it is dressed, etc. Therefore, there will be a lot of opportunities for brands, mainly to engage with the younger generation.

For some companies, especially those dealing with wearables and fashion, it might be easier to get involved in the avatar game. However, what about other brands? How does a food company make a metaverse play?

A brand like Chipotle can come in and say, "We're going to do a burrito, and we're going to give away $1 million worth of burritos in the game." These things are exciting and fun, and if the audience is engaged, they will enjoy it.

Obstacles to Overcome for Metaverse to Become More Mainstream

Hackl believes many things need to happen for metaverse to gain mainstream adoption. For example, only a tiny fraction of people today owns digital wallets. This is a generational problem since younger individuals understand digital ownership in ways older generations do not. These young individuals love to buy digital assets or spend on microtransactions. Once they get older, they may question things like, "Why can't I take this asset that I paid so much money for in Roblox and move it over to Fortnite?"

There is also a serious need for computing power. Unfortunately, as things stand, we have problems with supply chain issues related to chips, which slows things down. Education is also needed within organizations, and not just the brand teams, for everyone to understand where the metaverse space is headed.

AR & VR

CHAPTER TEN

AUGMENTED REALITY (AR) & VIRTUAL REALITY (VR)

When were virtual reality and augmented reality first introduced?

While primitive virtual reality systems got their start in the 1950s and 1960s, the concepts of VR and AR began to gain momentum in military applications during the early 1980s. Motion pictures such as Tron, The Matrix and Minority Report all offered futuristic riffs on how these technologies would evolve in the years to come.

The first mainstream attempt at releasing a VR headset was the Sega VR in 1993, an add-on to the Sega Genesis gaming system. While it never made it to market, it did stoke consumer interest in the technology. It would not be until the Oculus Rift in 2010 that a VR headset would be successful with a consumer audience — though today these devices remain expensive and largely of interest to niche, gaming-focused users.

Augmented reality splintered from virtual reality around 1990, and was brought to the public's attention in 1998, when TV broadcasters began overlaying a yellow line on the football field to better indicate the distance to a first down. Over the next decade, various apps around AR technology were designed for both military use (such as in fighter jet cockpits) and consumer use, when print magazines and packaged goods began embedding QR codes that could be scanned with a consumer's cell phone, making the product "come alive" with a short 3D video.

In 2014, Google rolled out Google Glass, with an eye toward equipping everyone with a head-mounted display AR device. The AR headset, which was controlled via voice and touch gestures, was met with skepticism and criticism, attributed to the new reality that people were recording video 24/7 in public. Privacy suddenly became a major talking point in consumer AR. Google ultimately suspended the project and relaunched it a few years later with enterprise users in mind.

What Are Augmented Reality and Virtual Reality?

Virtual Reality (VR) and **Augmented Reality (AR)** are two technologies that are changing the way we use screens, creating new and exciting interactive experiences.

Augmented Reality and **Virtual Reality** are reality technologies that either enhance or replace a real-life environment with a simulated one.

- **Augmented reality (AR)** augments your surroundings by adding digital elements to a live view, often by using the camera on a smartphone.
- **Virtual reality (VR)** is a completely immersive experience that replaces a real-life environment with a simulated one.

What is augmented reality or AR?

Integrating state-of-the-art technology can help keep your business competitive. With augmented reality (AR), you'll bridge the physical and digital worlds to better guide and train employees, solve problems faster, optimize efficiencies, improve productivity and collaboration, and better prepare for the future.

Understanding Augmented Reality

What is AR? Augmented reality is an enhanced, interactive version of a real-world environment achieved through digital visual elements, sounds, and other sensory stimuli via holographic technology. AR incorporates three features: a combination of digital and physical worlds, interactions made in real time, and accurate 3D identification of virtual and real objects.

Augmented reality offers a better way to design, curate, and deliver consumable instructions by overlaying digital content in real-world work environments. When a business understands what AR is and how to utilize it successfully, everyone can work remotely while collaborating efficiently

How Augmented Reality works

Augmented reality creates an immersive experience for all its users. Though the most common AR forms are through glasses or a camera lens, interest in AR is growing, and businesses are showcasing more types of lenses and hardware through the marketplace. There are five significant components of AR:

1. Artificial intelligence. Most augmented reality solutions need artificial intelligence (AI) to work, allowing users to complete actions using voice prompts. AI can also help process information for your AR application.

2. AR software. These are the tools and applications used to access AR. Some businesses can create their own form of AR software.

3. Processing. You'll need processing power for your AR technology to work, generally by leveraging your device's internal operating system.

4. Lenses. You'll need a lens or image platform to view your content or images. The better quality your screen is, the more realistic your image will appear.

5. Sensors. AR systems need to digest data about their environment to align the real and digital worlds. When your camera captures information, it sends it through software for processing.

Integrating AR into your employee training and education

In the workplace, adding augmented reality to your processes and procedures can help enhance the learning and comprehension benefits for your employees. AR training is an educational experience presented through the software on AR devices to help employees gain critical professional skills. This type of training experience can be launched at any time, any place with the right software.

AR can also help guide and support employees regardless of their location, leading to better collaboration and safer working conditions in your fields. By enhancing traditional learning methods, this method can offer more information for better comprehension. Some ways your team could use AR would be:

- Performance support
- Learning and training modules
- New hire onboarding
- On-demand training opportunities
- Customer service and experience

How is augmented reality being used in business?

Many industries and sectors already use AR for business processes, include with examples:

- **Retail.** Employees can use AR for onboarding and training sessions. It helps new employees in their future transactions, such as sales training, touring the sales floor, and preparing for a retail environment. AR can also help customers test products before purchasing or learn how to use them within their environments. This can create better engagement or help customers solve problems by providing actionable information in a real-world context.
- **Manufacturing.** Technology can offer step-by-step instructions, allowing trainers to provide feedback during practice for better retention. Using mixed reality also enables employees to learn while on the job, keeping their hands free to perform work.
- **Healthcare.** Getting hands-on experience in performing procedures without risk is imperative for healthcare professionals. AR provides the guidance to practically, yet safely, learn about anatomy and surgeries.
- **Military.** AR is integrated in combat training to stimulate situational and operational environments so soldiers have awareness of their time, space, and forces.
- **Automobile.** AR can help train and allow specialists to explore current and future models, along with their internal systems.

- **Design and construction.** Arguably the most common and fruitful application for AR today, designers are using augmented reality to see what hypothetical products (or structures) look like in real environments and to make virtual tweaks to existing products without ever laying a hand on them.
- **Maintenance and repairs.** AR technology can guide technicians through the steps of repairing, upgrading, and maintaining a wide range of products, ranging from industrial equipment to entire buildings. AR allows technicians to work on equipment without having to refer to printed manuals or websites, overlaying detailed instructions – often visual – atop the machinery itself.
- **Training and education.** Businesses are using AR technology to provide an immersive experience when training employees, allowing them to more comprehensively visualize new products and concepts. Schools are following suit.

Besides industry-specific uses, many industries currently use AR apps to identify, track, and resolve technical issues. It can also help in other non-physical procedure cases like for marketing as a advertising,

entertainment, and events tool by allowing users to get information simply through their phones.

In deciding which type of AR technology you'll need for your business, you'll first have to determine what kind of AR to use. There are two types of augmented reality: marker-based and marker-less. Choosing one of these types of AR will determine how you'll be able to display your images and information.

Types of Augmented Reality

In deciding which type of AR technology you'll need for your business, you'll first have to determine what kind of AR to use. There are two types of augmented reality: marker-based and marker-less. Choosing one of these types of AR will determine how you'll be able to display your images and information.

Marker-based AR is created using image recognition to identify objects already programmed into your AR device or application. When placing objects in view as points of reference, they can help your AR device determine the position and orientation of the camera. This is generally achieved by switching your camera to grayscale and detecting a marker to compare that marker with all the others in its information bank. Once your device finds a match, it uses that data to mathematically determine the pose and place the AR image in the right spot.

Marker-less AR is more complex as there's no point in which your device will focus on. Because of this, your device must recognize items as they appear in view. Using a recognition algorithm, the device will look for colors, patterns, and similar features to determine what that object is and then, using time, accelerometer, GPS, and compass information, it will or orient itself and use a camera to overlay an image of whatever you'd like within your real-world surroundings.

Virtual Reality (AR)

Virtual Reality (VR), the use of computer modeling and simulation that enables a person to interact with an artificial three-dimensional (3-D) visual or other sensory environment. VR applications immerse the user in a computer-generated environment that simulates reality through the use of interactive devices, which send and receive information and are worn as goggles, headsets, gloves, or body suits. In a typical VR format, a user wearing a helmet with a stereoscopic screen views animated images of a simulated environment. The illusion of "being there" (telepresence) is effected by motion sensors that pick up the user's movements and adjust the view on the screen accordingly, usually in real time (the instant the user's movement takes place). Thus, a user can tour a simulated suite of rooms, experiencing changing viewpoints and perspectives that are convincingly related to his own head turnings and steps. Wearing data gloves equipped with force-feedback devices that provide the sensation of touch, the user can even pick up and manipulate objects that he sees in the virtual environment.

The 3 Types of Virtual Reality

Virtual reality is a fully digital, computer-generated, three-dimensional experiential environment. Unlike traditional user interfaces that only allow users to view a screen, VR allows the user to step inside an experience, to be immersed in and interact with a 3D world that can either simulate or differ completely from the real world. (Related: augmented reality medical training, VR medical training, AR + VR medical education)

By simulating the senses as possible – such as vision, hearing, and sometimes touch – a computer is transformed into a gatekeeper to a new world. The only limits to a VR experience are the availability of content and computing power.

There are 3 primary categories of virtual reality simulations used today: non-immersive, semi-immersive, and fully-immersive simulations.

NON-IMMERSIVE VIRTUAL REALITY

Non-immersive virtual experiences are often overlooked as a virtual reality category because it's already so commonly used in everyday life. This technology provides a computer-generated environment, but allows the user to stay aware of and keep control of their physical environment. Non-immersive virtual reality systems rely on a computer or video game console, display, and input devices like keyboards, mice, and controller. A video game is a great example of a non-immersive VR experience.

SEMI-IMMERSIVE VIRTUAL REALITY

Semi-immersive virtual experiences provide users with a partially virtual environment. It will still give users the perception of being in a different reality when they focus on the digital image, but also allows users to remain connected to their physical surroundings. Semi-immersive technology provides realism through through 3D graphics, a term known as vertical reality depth. More detailed graphics result in a more immersive feeling. This category of VR is used often for educational or training purposes and relies on high-resolution displays, powerful computers, projectors or hard simulators that partially replicate design and functionality of functional real-world mechanisms.

FULLY IMMERSIVE VIRTUAL REALITY

Fully-immersive simulations give users the most realistic simulation experience, complete with sight and sound. To experience and interact with fully-immersive virtual reality, the user needs the proper VR glasses or a head mount display (HMD). VR headsets provide high-resolution content with a wide field of view. The display typically splits between the user's eyes, creating a stereoscopic 3D effect, and combines with input tracking to establish an immersive, believable experience. This type of VR has been commonly adapted for gaming and other entertainment purposes, but usage in other sectors, namely education, is increasing now as well. The possibilities for VR usage are endless.

The Difference Between AR and VR

Virtual reality and augmented reality accomplish two very different things in two very different ways, despite their devices' similar designs. VR replaces reality, taking you somewhere else. AR adds to reality, projecting information on top of what you're already seeing. They're both powerful technologies that have yet to make their mark with consumers, but show a lot of promise. They can completely change how we use computers in the future,

Jobs in the VR and AR Industry

These new, evolving technologies produce endless opportunities for businesses and employment—By 2022, the AR and VR market is projected to grow to $209.2 billion. VR and AR are transforming industries through software and hardware development, graphic design, research, and more.

In-demand careers developing and improving VR and AR technology include:

- Software engineering and development
- Project management
- Software maintenance
- Graphic design

WEB 3.0

CHAPTER ELEVEN

WHAT IS WEB 3?

What is Web 3?

The web 3.0 revolution will utilize decentralized protocols such as blockchain, the technology used to facilitate cryptocurrency transactions. By addressing the key issues of data ownership and control, it hopes to address some of the major setbacks and shortcomings of the current internet age.

Let's take a look at things from a different perspective.

Today, a huge portion of the world's population relies heavily on internet-related services provided by big technology companies. Unlike Google, Apple, and Amazon, these companies dictate what services their users can use and act as middlemen between their users and their wants.

However, Web3 operates on a decentralized network and doesn't require permission. In other words, internet providers do not have the authority to impose their will on who uses their services. They also do not serve as intermediaries between users and their needs.

Core Components of Web3

•

Blockchain Network

Blockchain technology is one of Web3's key features. Decentralization is at the heart of web 3 which is built upon blockchain technology. With blockchain technology, data is decentralized, open, and can be distributed. So users own their data and are free to trade them without worrying about losing ownership, losing privacy, or depending on intermediaries. In addition, it allows you to log in securely over the Internet without being tracked by anyone.

Also, the use of blockchain-based tokens and cryptocurrencies in Web3 are important aspects of the potential internet era. Among other things, users can earn rewards for their contributions to the platform's growth by transparently monetizing and contributing to online upgrades.

•

Artificial Intelligence

As a result of the advancement of artificial intelligence, useful predictions can now be made, and sometimes even lifesaving actions can be taken. In spite of the fact that Web 2.0 has had its share of AI, it is still largely human-driven as long as the big tech companies control the majority of internet traffic.

It is therefore inevitable that corrupt behaviors, such as biased product reviews, rigged ratings of some internet services, and human errors will continue to exist. Customers are able to leave feedback on most internet review services. It is unfortunate that companies sometimes hire large groups of people to write excellent product or service evaluations.

In reverse, people may be paid to rate poorly and write negative reviews of an app or service. It is the goal of Web 3.0 to reduce the incidence of such manipulations. Artificial Intelligence is a key component of the internet since it assists in distinguishing between legitimate and fraudulent actions, thereby providing more accurate information to users.

•

AR and VR

In a metaverse, users work, learn, play, entertain, and play games with other people. Based on a variety of technologies, but mostly on Virtual Reality (VR) and Augmented Reality (AR).

The company's blockchain projects make use of fungible (dividendable and exchangeable) tokens that are used to buy digital assets of the world like virtual land or outfits for avatars. Metaverse is still at an infant stage and hasn't been fully developed. Internet users and technologists see great potential in this technology even at that level.

What follows is a list of many people's future metaverse-related expectations;

- Metaverse technology is a core feature of Web3 and will be built using blockchain systems and open standards, and it will be run by a network of computers around the world rather than a single entity.
- In order to build some Web3 applications, the following three technologies will be used: augmented reality, virtual reality, and holographic projections.
- A non-fungible token (NFT) will be used to facilitate virtual reality transactions.
- The traditional gatekeepers would not be able to restrict access to the metaverse.

What are the key characteristics of Web3?

Self-governing, stateful, robust, and with native built-in payments, Web3 is self-governing. It exhibits the following characteristics –

- **Decentralized**

Web3 data is stored in blockchain, so no single system has access to it all. It is dispersed across multiple platforms. This facilitates decentralized access and increases the chances of failure.

- **Permissionless**

The Internet can be accessed by users without requiring special permissions in Web3. Users will not need to disclose their personal information to access specific services. There will be no need to compromise privacy or share any other information.

- **Secure**

Unlike Web 2.0, Web 3.0 is more secure since decentralization makes it more difficult for hackers to target specific databases.

What Is The Use Of Web3?

Decentralized applications run on a blockchain can be referred to as Web3 in the context of Ethereum. Participation in these apps is free of charge and your personal information is not monetized.

As part of this next generation of the internet, blockchain technology and cryptocurrency are used to promote decentralization. The Web 3.0 platform is designed to give users access to their own data. As a result, individuals will be able to provide services to each other and control the aspects of the internet that they use without having to rely on the big tech companies.

Some examples of web3 applications are:

Bitcoin: World's largest cryptocurrency is a perfect example of a decentralized transaction.

Apple Siri: Perfect example for Web3(Web 3.0).In the year since Siri of the 4s model, the AI assistant gave more expanded capabilities. Siri is a complicated and personalized platform by using speech recognition and AI tech.

Opensea: It is a blockchain-based marketplace for purchasing and selling NFTs.

Google Cloud: The tech giant announced to beef up Web3 into a cloud system.

Difference of Web3 and Metaverse

- **Objective**

A major advancement of web2, the Web3 is the next-generation technology that wants a democratic and decentralized internet environment. An individual user can be an owner or shareholder, not a tech giant. In web3, the user neither needs permission nor to follow predetermined rules. The Metaverse system wants to establish a 3d world or Virtual reality for users.

- **Application**

Remember that Web 3.0 is the process engine that uses the blockchain's advances. Metaverse is a new dimension that includes health, game, film, concert, entertainment, social platforms, education, virtual training techniques that employ Web 3.0 tech advances to achieve their target.

- **Fundamental difference**

The Metaverse is home to several critical technologies that help run the entire ecosystem. To build the Metaverse, connection, interfaces, decentralization, a creator economy, and advanced technology are all required.

The target of Web 3.0 is to create a decentralized web-based only on the blockchain. Users can connect with online services using blockchain, governed by a decentralized peer-to-peer network world.

- **Portraits of Metaverse and Web3**

Of course, the critical point of comparison is the portraits of web 3.0 and Metaverse. The metaverse is a 3D world where you can interact with 3D friends, objects, places. For example, you can play games with your friends from the creator's ground. In the case of Web3, the users can cultivate, own, sell, buy their content. In addition, users can charge their creations.

- **Perception of different ways**

While Web 3.0 is primarily concerned with who will rule(tech giants or individuals) and govern the internet in the future, the Metaverse is concerned with how users will interact with it. A large section of people now use computers, smartphones, and tablets to navigate websites and to access apps. Proponents of the Metaverse believe that we will utilize Virtual Reality (VR) technology to enter the internet tomorrow, navigating between virtual realms as digital avatars.

By making use of the blockchain system for both of them one after another, data is owned, open,well-distributed, and collectively owned by peer-to-peer networks but it is different in the case where one can find to do business through VR, another helps contributors to own their data.

- **Basic Technology**

Let's make a set of basic technology behind the web3 process; blockchain, decentralized autonomous organization, and cryptocurrency. The crypto body emerged as the world's first decentralized step towards web3. On the other hand, the Metaverse is built upon the basis of augmented reality, Human interface, edge computing, creator economy, NFTs, Multitasking UI,5g, and wifi 6g(at the budding stage).

- **Ownership battle**

The objective of web3 is to keep the internet out of the monopoly of tech giants and make it public-controlled property. The most successful examples are the crypto world bitcoin market.

On the other hand, tech mammoths are starting reformation or trying to acquire metaverse firms to control this world already. However, experts assured that public internet control would make it tough for corporations to own the meta world.

CHAPTER TWELVE

WEB 3.0 – THE EVOLUTION OF THE INTERNET

The internet has undergone significant change since it was invented. From the Internet Relay Chat (IRC) to modern social media, it is now a vital part of human interactions, and is still evolving.

Web 3.0 is the next generation of Internet technology that mainly relies on machine learning and artificial intelligence (AI). It aims to create more open, connected, and intelligent websites and web applications that focus on a machine-based understanding of data.

Web 3.0 aims to provide more personalized and relevant information through AI and advanced machine learning techniques at a faster rate. This can be achieved through using smarter algorithms and the development of Big Data analytics.

Currently, most websites have static information or user-driven content, such as forums and social media. While this allows information to be published to a broad group of people, it may not cater to the specific needs of users. A website should tailor the information it provides to each user, similar to the dynamism of real-world human communication.

Tim Bernes-Lee, a computer scientist, provided a succinct explanation about a Semantic Web in 1999. "I have a dream for the Web [in which computers] become capable of analyzing all the data on the Web - the content links and transactions between people and computers." A "Semantic Web," which makes this possible, has yet to emerge, but when it does, the day-to-day mechanism of trade, bureaucracy, and your daily lives will be handled by machines talking to machines.

In Web 3.0, an ocean of information can be accessed from websites and applications, and they can understand and use the data in a meaningful manner to the user.

Brief Overview of The Internet's Revolution

Websites and web applications have changed dramatically over the last decades. They have evolved from static sites to data-driven sites that users can interact with and influence.

Web 1.0

The first internet was referred to as Web 1.0, a term coined by Darci DiNucci, an author and designer. Back in the early 90s, websites were built using static HTML pages that could only display information - users could not change the data.

Web 2.0

That changed during the late 90s, when the shift towards a more interactive internet started taking form. Web 2.0 users could interact with websites through databases, server-side processing, forms, and social media.

This brought forth a change from a static to more dynamic web. Web 2.0 brought an increased emphasis on user-generated content and interoperability between different sites and applications. Web 2.0 was less about observation and more about participation. By the mid-2000s, most websites made the transition to Web 2.0.

The Future

When looking at the internet's history, the evolution of a more semantically intelligent web makes sense. Data was first statically presented to users. Then users could dynamically interact with that data. Algorithms can use all that data to improve user experience and make the web more personalized and familiar.

Web 3.0, while not fully defined, could leverage Peer-to-Peer (P2P) technologies such as Blockchain, open-source software, virtual reality, the Internet of Things, and more.

Currently, most applications can only run on a single operating system. Web 3.0 enables applications to be more device-agnostic, meaning they could run on various types of hardware and software without any added development costs.

Additionally, Web 3.0 aims to make the internet more open and decentralized. In the current framework, users can only rely on network and cellular providers that survey the information going through their system. With the advent of distributed ledger technologies, that may soon change, and users can take back ownership of their data.

What Makes Web 3.0 Superior to Its Predecessors?

- Decentralization of control - since intermediaries are removed from the equation, user data will no longer be controlled by them. This reduces the risk of censorship by governments or corporations and cuts down the effectiveness of Denial-of-Service (DoS) attacks.

- Increased information interconnectivity - As more products become connected to the internet, larger data sets provide algorithms with more information to analyze. This can help them provide more accurate information that accommodates the specific needs of the individual user.

- More efficient browsing - When using search engines, finding the best results used to be quite challenging. However, over the years, they have become better at finding semantically relevant results based on search context and metadata. This results in a more convenient web browsing experience that can help anyone find the exact information they need with relative ease.

- Improved advertising and marketing - No one likes being bombarded with online ads. Web 3.0 aims to improve advertising by leveraging smarter AI systems and targeting specific audiences based on consumer data.

The internet's evolution has come a long way from non-editable information to a web that provides a considerably better user experience. While there is no concrete definition for Web 3.0 yet, innovations in other technological fields are already set in motion.

CHAPTER THIRTEEN

THE EVOLVEMENT OF WEB 3

Web 3 has attracted a lot of attention to the dramatic changes it will bring to the industry, but few know exactly what it will bring and how it will happen. To understand this, it is necessary to go back in time and examine its predecessors, Web 1 and 2.

Remember Web 1?

Just like the middle-age, Web 1 wasn't named until the dust settled. As we all know, the 'World Wide Web' is just a set of static websites displaying a lot of information and no interactive content. Connection means dialing through a wobbly modem and preventing anyone from using the phone in the house. It is a network of AOL chat rooms and MSN Messenger, AltaVista and Ask Jeeves. It's excruciatingly slow. Streaming video and music? Forget it. It takes at least a day to download a song.

Here comes Web 2 ?

The memory of creepy modems and boring interfaces is largely gone. Faster internet speeds have paved the way for interactive content, and the web is no longer for observation, but for engagement. Global information sharing gave birth to the age of 'social media'. YouTube, Wikipedia, Flickr and Facebook give voice to the voiceless and prosper like-minded communities.

We might call it the era of 'literacy' - the dissemination of information is as simple as it could be. So here comes the question, if web 2 is actually so great, what went wrong?

Information is a money

The United Nations estimates that between the year 2000 and 2015, the number of Internet users rose from 738 million to 3.2 billion. Large digital companies realize personal information is an invaluable asset hidden in a marvelous amount of data. So they began to store data in large quantities on centralized servers, with Amazon, Facebook and Twitter being the biggest hosts. People sacrifice security of their data for the convenience provided by these services. Whether they know it or not, their identities, browsing habits, searches, and online shopping information are sold to the highest bidders.

The Revolutionary Web 3

The vision for a fairer and more transparent web dates back to around 2006, but at the time there were no tools and technologies that could make it happen. Then Bitcoin brought the concept of a distributed ledger or blockchain for peer-to-peer digital storage. Decentralization is an idea, and blockchain the means. Now we have what is called a human-centric internet.

A antitrust network for privacy

While Web 2 has democratized many power structures and created new opportunities, the economic engine is largely privatized and monopolized. Facebook, Uber and AirBnB have created private networks for the public infrastructure they dominate. Web 3, on the contrary, is about multiple profit centers sharing value through an open web.

It is imaginable that in the near future, cryptocurrency-based mobile phones, VPNs, decentralized storage and cryptocurrency wallets will be widely available. We don't need network and cellular providers that suspend or monitor our information in the future. These are the tools we need if we are to avoid sleepwalking into a Black-Mirror- style privacy dystopia. Web 3 comes with many advantages:

1. No central point of control : The middleman is removed and blockchains like Ethereum provide a trust-less platform where rules are unbreakable and data is fully encrypted. Alphabet and Apple can no longer control users' data. No government or entity has the power to kill websites and services, nor can no one's identities be controlled by others.

2. Ownership of data:

Ultimately, users will regain full control over their data and have the security of encryption. Information can then be shared on a case-by-case and permission basis. Currently, big companies like Amazon and Facebook have server factories that store information such as dietary preferences, income, interests, credit card details and more, and it's not just about improving their services - marketers and advertisers pay billions of dollars a year for the data.

3. Significant reduction in hacking and data breaches:

As data is fragmented and distributed, hackers will need to shut down entire networks, and state-backed tools such as Vault7 will be obsolete. Nowadays, internet companies are forced to hand over users' data or submit to the censorship of entire databases. These data breaches are not limited to major security threats such as terrorism– in 2017, Coinbase took the IRS to court for access to data on more than 15,000 of its customers.

This case, which Coinbase ultimately lost, paved the way for government entities to take over the finances of thousands of customers, with few good reasons to justify the intrusion. Unfortunately, such cases are not isolated. In 2013, secure email provider Lavabit chose to shut down rather than hand over its SSL keys to the US government for its spying on Edward Snowden.

4. Interoperability: Apps will be easily customizable and device-agnostic, able to run on smartphones, TVs, cars, microwave ovens and smart sensors. Currently, applications are OS-specific and generally limited to a single operational system. For example, many Android cryptocurrency wallets are not available on iO, frustrating consumers with multiple devices, increasing the cost of developers who are responsible for releasing multiple iterations and updates of the software.

5. Permissionless Blockchain : Anyone can create addresses and interact with the network. The ability to access permissionless chains cannot be overemphasized. Users are not banned for their geography, income, gender, orientation, or many other sociological and demographic factors. Wealth and other digital assets can be transferred across borders quickly and efficiently anywhere in the world.

6. Uniterrupted Service : Account suspensions and distributed denial of service are significantly reduced. Without any single point failure, service disruption will be minimal. Data will be stored on distributed nodes to ensure redundancy, and multiple backups will prevent servers from failing or being occupied.

How does it operate?

Just like any emerging technology, it's still being perfected. In order to access the decentralized web, one only needs a seed as a single asset that can interact with dApps and other services. Individuals can still use a web browser to access the Internet, and it will visually be Web-2-user-friendly.

On the surface, the learning curve from 2 to 3 will be flat and smooth. But behind the scenes, their frameworks that connect users to digital services are quite different. In web 3, transactions are manually signed and verified to prevent platforms from stealing personal information without a valid reason. Web users will opt in, rather than try—and often fail—to opt out.

New platforms will emerge and the level of competition will not be limited by monopoly service providers. Here is the concept: the decentralized applications, wallets, platforms, and other digital assets that currently make up Web 3 are decentralized. Accessing these interfaces requires separate seeds, logins and identities —much like the existing Web 2. Through a single seed, Essentia.one will link these different platforms together. This will operate as an encryption key that can be associated with its owner, and Essentia will provide proof of identity without giving up any unnecessary personal identity.

Just as Web 2 did not automatically wipe out Web 1 (which still collects dust around some parts of the Internet), the migration to web 3 will take time for its integration with existing online systems. The wheels have rolled on and the train has left the station. Web 3 is a movement revolution, and we have passed the point of no return.

CHAPTER FOURTEEN

THE FUTURE PATH OF WEB 3

Now is about time to launch the next iteration of the internet, smart, as decentralized digital services are powered by blockchain and the new technology Waves is building.

In fact, the concept of decentralization is fairly new. Surprisingly, it was first formulated around the 19th century along with the concept of centralization itself. Before that, people hadn't really thought about the general principles of what they built, be it social structure or technology. The creation of giant nation-states draws attention to the general principles of social structure and raises suspicions that rigid vertical structures have their own drawbacks. Strict hierarchies and chains of command do make sense in many cases, but they always come with centralized points of failure, leaving the system open to attack and breach.

In the late 20th century, technology began its overwhelming impact on social development. Computer networks become the blood vessels of the society; the technologies we have built have a huge impact on the society we live in. The concept of decentralized technology began to take shape in the late 1970s, in the form of distributed computing and consensus research.

The real breakthrough comes from blockchain technology. For the first time in the history of human technology, we are able to create truly decentralized systems controlled by the protocols we enter. Blockchain is now over 10 years old, and while we can't do everything we want with it yet, we can do enough to try and move beyond prototypes and working use cases. Massive adoption is the holy grail of any emerging technology and must be found soon because the time has come. WEB2 companies have already wielded too much power. For a long time we didn't notice how they achieved a massive volume of sensitive and valuable big data, but now the monopoly cannot last.

WEB3, a concept that emerged at the end of the last century, finally took shape in the first real products that unify many different technologies (big data, artificial intelligence, IoT...) on a decentralized basis . To start the revolution, it is crucial to create WEB3.0 retail products and working enterprise applications. We need to look beyond the crypto community and make ideas that emerge within it really work.

We are not yet fully decentralized, and in fact we probably never will be. In order to make WEB3 a truly useful concept, we need to understand that the ultimate goal of WEB3 is to create robust, transparent and collaborative systems by any means necessary. By decentralizing critical business logics and using centralized technology where it is inevitable (storage, complex computing), we are able to create products of massive current adoption, and put things in the place where a new approach is actually needed in our current systems. Data storage can be enhanced and privacy protection be allowed. It's time to start working on some fancy and complicated cryptography like homomorphic encryption, and really make it work. In the near future, I'm sure we'll be able to use verifiable computation as well.

Certainly the decentralization layer must be improved to address the scalability issues currently plaguing blockchain systems. Future systems may (and probably should) abandon network-wide synchronization entirely, but there is still a long way to go.

The next architectural level is the decentralized business logic layer. Sensitive business logic running on smart contracts, encrypting important private data, monetizing through tokenization - it's all there. Going a little deeper, we reach the centralization layer, which also absorbs the idea of WEB3 - data is encrypted and computation is verifiable.

Based on this architecture, Waves has built several applications with mass adoption:

These applications taps into diverse markets, but are unified through the idea of tokenization, making them accessible to the masses and providing unparalleled transparency.

A decentralized voting platform is built. This is one of the most promising directions of distributed technology. Its use at the municipal level has emerged — and its widespread use is inevitable. Transparent, anonymous and verifiable voting can be a game changer.

A social network is built. This is an ambitious move at an appropriate moment. Privacy-preserving, tokenized social networks could be a giant leap in social interaction.

The Vostok Network they launched is a solution for enterprise WEB3. By default, any implementation of blockchain technology in the enterprise is WEB3, as it only makes sense in an enterprise environment to combine different technologies on a decentralized basis. Without it, the blockchain is just a weird database.

CHAPTER FIFTEEN

WHY WEB 3.0 MATTERS

Why Web 3.0 Matters

The web has come a long way in just a few years, and has greatly improved how people communicate and do business. Thanks to continued innovations, the web has seen some significant evolutions.

Web1, which roughly dates between 1990 -2005, was about open protocols that were decentralized and community governed. Most of the value were accrued to edges of the network, who are mostly users and builders. The following 15 years would see the rise of Web2 (2005-2020), which was siloed, and made up of centralized services run by corporations. In this version of the web, most of the value were accrued to a handful of companies like Google, Apple, Amazon, and Facebook. If you have been paying attention to our timeline, we are now commencing on the era of Web3. This web combines the decentralization and community-governed ethos of Web1 with the advanced, modern functionality of Web2. This new web is owned by the builders and users, and orchestrated with tokens.

Why Web 3.0 Matters

To understand why this new web matters, you need to understand the problems with centralized platforms, for which there are many. For starters, centralized platforms follow a predictable life cycle. At first, they will do everything they can to recruit users and third-party complements like creators, developers, and businesses. The goal is to strengthen their network effect. As these platforms move up the adoption S-curve, their power over users and third parties steadily grows.

When they hit the top of the S-curve, their relationship with network participants changes from positive-sum to zero-sum. The only way they can continue to grow is by extracting data from users and competing with (former) partners. There are many examples here, such as Epic vs. Apple, Facebook vs. Zynga, Microsoft vs. Netscape, Google vs. Yelp, and Twitter vs. its third-party clients.

You can imagine how it feels for third parties where their relationship with these corporations goes from cooperation to competition. Due to this devious strategy, over time, the best entrepreneurs, developers, and investors have learned not to build on top of centralized platforms, which generally attempts to stifle innovation.

Enter Web 3.0

In Web3, ownership and control are decentralized. This allows users and builders to own pieces of internet services by holding tokens that can be both fungible and non-fungible (NFTs). It is shaping to be a token-based internet, where token holders get property rights such as the ability to own a piece of the internet.

For example, NFTs allow users to own objects, such as art, music, code, photos, text, game objects, governance rights, credentials, access passes, and whatever else people can think of. NFTs live on blockchains such as Ethereum, a decentralized network owned and operated by its users. Most blockchains are public, allowing anyone with a computer to participate in a network. They are also decentralized, meaning no one owns them.

Ethereum, for its part, is powered by a fungible token, Ether (ETH), that is used to incentivize the physical computers that underlie the system. ETH is also used for transactions on its network, such as to make NFT purchases.

Why Is There So Much Hype Around Web3?

Most of the excitement surrounding Web3 comes from the crypto community that benefits from an internet that is more decentralized. Also, companies such as Reddit have created some buzz around the term, as they plan to start developing Web3 services and platforms.

Many experts speculate that Web3 could augment video games, for example, by allowing players to more easily buy and sell in-game items, or give them more power to determine how the game is run. However, the biggest buzz has stemmed from the Metaverse narrative.

Metaverse essentially refers to a future internet consisting of three-dimensional spaces in a virtual reality where users can interact. It will be fully immersive, something along the lines of the movie Ready Player One. A few companies have been quick to lay claim to the metaverse, such as Facebook, who recently changed its name to Meta. However, some technologists hope that Web3 will incubate a metaverse built using blockchain systems and open standards, and run by a network of computers worldwide, rather than a few big companies.

Meta, on its part, believes the metaverse will not be created by one company, and it will establish a "massively larger creative economy than the one constrained by today's platforms and their policies."

Whether this statement is to be trusted is another thing, given that Facebook has fought hard over the years to maintain its dominance within the social media space. It is clear they are striving to be a powerful institution, even in the coming Web3 era.

However, proponents of decentralization should take heart as NFTs will facilitate commerce within Web3. This means that traditional gatekeepers will not be able to dictate what can and cannot go into the metaverse.

CHAPTER SIXTEEN

THE DIFFERENCE BETWEEN WEB 2.0 AND WEB 3.0

If you are familiar with the internet of today, you know what Web2 is: an internet dominated by companies that provide services in exchange for your personal data. On the other hand, Web3 represents the next evolution of the internet. While we still do not have a clear definition of Web3, it is possible to paint a picture of what it will be about thanks to the existence of crypto projects.

Purpose of Web 3

Today, the internet or Web2 is controlled by big tech companies such as Google, Amazon, Netflix, YouTube and Meta, formerly known as Facebook. These companies hold the information, power and all the profits associated with their users' data. However, Web3 plans to steer us away from this tyranny through decentralization, where we will get a share of the profits. Today, the most viable way to achieve this goal is through blockchain technology and decentralized applications.

Brief History of the Internet

The first generation of the internet (Web1) constituted a stream of information, and existed from 1991-2004. It was known as the read-only web and allowed the broadcast of information to users.

Web1 was made up of static web pages and did not feature many content creators. Even though it was revolutionary for its time, interaction and functionality were rather limited.

Web2 saw a stream of interaction. It is the internet as we know it today, which is less static and more dynamic. This version of the internet became more popular in 2004 when the first Web2 conference took place. The system behind this web aimed to actively engage users, with the content itself becoming more user-generated. Web2 components like blogs, wikis and social media platforms have changed how we share and deliver information. For example, Facebook and Twitter allow users to share their thoughts, perspectives and opinions by liking, sharing, tagging, tweeting, etc. Even though there is a dependency on big tech companies to provide the infrastructure and services needed, Web3 hopes to eliminate this reliance.

Web3 will be a stream of interpretation. The next version of the internet will be more intelligent, autonomous and open. This means that computers will be able to interpret information in a way that is more similar to humans and by using technologies such as blockchain, artificial intelligence (AI), augmented reality (AR) and virtual reality (VR), providing users with more personalized content and experiences.

Potential Benifits of Web3

Personalization: Thanks to Web3, the internet experience will likely become more customized for the user, allowing for more efficient search, relevant marketing, better communication, and increased information linking.

Secure peer-to-peer (P2P) network: Web3 will allow users to connect, transact and share data privately without relying on third parties. This is unlike Web2, where every time you interact with the internet, copies of your data get sent to the data servers, and you no longer own it exclusively.

Ownership of information, data and digital assets: By using blockchain technology, Web3 aims to displace tech giants by handing complete ownership of data back to the users. In this Web2 era, big tech companies such as Amazon and Facebook store your data and personal information, mostly to improve their marketing and analytics. However, many privacy concerns have been raised over such one-sided data governance, and many see Web3 as the solution.

Permissionless: Another way Web3 promises to provide a more democratic system is that there will be no restrictions on who can be part of the network. Also, neither users nor suppliers will require authorization from a governing body to participate. This means that services are available to everyone, and individuals can influence the network based on their value.

More democracy and involvement: Web3 will allow users to be more involved in future ecosystem developments. As a result, the ecosystems will not have presidents or CEOs but Decentralized Autonomous Organizations (DAOs), where token owners have a say in changes and developments.

Censorship resistance: Unlike Web2 platforms that store data on centralized servers, Web3 is decentralized. This means its servers cannot be accessed, altered or removed by any party such as corporations, governments or hackers. Also, these entities cannot deny users access to services since blockchain-related technologies such as IPFS and distributed hash tables can form a content system that is much more difficult to block and takedown.

Digital Identity: Another awesome thing about Web3 is that everyone will have their own digital identity and more control over their privacy. Progress in the development of Web3 means a decentralized digital identity for everyone is becoming a possibility.

All in all, Web3 will be about utilizing blockchain and many other decentralized protocols, such as data oracles, storage, messaging and digital identities. However, technological advancements in decentralized systems will not mean that the internet will look any different. Less technical users might not even see the difference, since web3's innovation is most noticeable at the "backend" of the internet. Thus, you can expect to see decentralized versions of the same apps you are used to without significant differences.

CHAPTER SEVENTEEN

HOW TO MEASURE GROWTH IN WEB3

More and more Web3 projects are aiming to build decentralized versions of existing Web2 platforms and services. For example, a protocol such as Compound is building the Web3 version of the Bank of America, while Uniswap is essentially a decentralized version of the NYSE. Meanwhile, Yearn Finance serves as a decentralized version of Blackrock.

Today, there are thousands of Web3 projects that promise to be open-source, permissionless, and supported by token economies. While most of them label themselves as decentralized networks, protocols, DAOs and dApps, they are simply businesses with products that will fail to grow if they do not view themselves as such.

Crypto is rampant with ideology, but at the end of the day, ideology does not pay the bills. Projects assigning terms such as "protocol" and "DAO" are still required to develop and scale a product that people actually want to use. Also, there is an uphill task for Web3 projects to develop something better than their existing Web2 counterparts, which means making up for the significant UX friction of using a product with a crypto backend. These projects also need to acknowledge that while owning your own data may be critical to a small percentage of your users, most of them are compelled by convenience, not privacy.

Until recently, most projects have been judged by their token's price and market cap, which can are largely speculative by nature.This is not a great proxy for long-term success. Below, let us explore some useful Web3-native growth metrics. They apply to three major categories: DeFi, Layer 1s/Layer 2s, and Play-to-Earn Gaming.

DeFi

When it comes to DeFi, value growth can be tracked through financial inflows and integrations. Today, some examples of DeFi apps include decentralized exchanges such as Uniswap and lending protocols like Compound. Many of these DeFi projects are developed by a centralized development team that eventually distributes management of its operations to a decentralized community of token holders. To assess the value growth of these protocols, you can check out these indicators:

Total Value Locked – TVL has been the number one measure of success for DeFi apps. It represents the cumulative value of crypto assets deposited by users on the protocol for trading, staking, and lending. While it might be a great metric for borrowing/lending protocols such as Aave and Compound, it is not that useful for DEXs like Uniswap that measure growth primarily by trading volume. TVL may have its drawbacks in measuring long-term growth, given that users and traders will jump from one protocol to another in search of higher yield. Also, a few whales can create the illusion of activity, ultimately making TVL unreliable. That said, TVL remains a good metric to inspire confidence in protocols as assets locked have tangible value and bear an opportunity cost for other productive uses.

Active Wallets - used to measure the Daily Active Wallets and Monthly Active Wallets. A rising number means the app is seeing more activities - buying, selling, staking, etc.

Number of Integrations – since DeFi apps have the ability to interact with and build on other DeFi apps, the number and quality of integrations can be used to measure growth. This means assessing the number of wallets, exchanges, and DeFi products willing to integrate with the app.

Layer 1s and Layer 2s

Layer 1 stands for base-level blockchains like Ethereum, Near, Avalanche, Flow, etc. In contrast, Layer 2 represents projects such as Polygon that sit on top of existing Layer 1s that helps with scaling. A few ways to measure growth for these protocols include:

The number of developers and applications - Growth is measured through developer activity when it comes to Layer 1s and Layer 2s. Projects in this spectrum are open-source, meaning anyone can build on top of them and integrate with them. This means the number of developers and apps built on top of a given protocol represents the most important growth metric. GitHub is a good resource to assess developer activity.

The number of active wallets - As was the case with DeFi projects, the number of active daily and monthly users can offer some insight into the growth of the L1/L2 protocols.

Total number and size of transactions – another growth metric in this category is the number of transactions, the number of large transactions (over $100,000), and the transaction volume of a given protocol. It offers insight into the network's use as a means of exchange, even though it is not the end goal for most projects.

Play- to- Earn Gaming

For P2E gaming, growth can be accessed through partnerships and player incentives. P2E games allow players to receive rewards with real-world value. Unlike regular video games where in-game items are held on private data networks and owned by the game creators, NFTs allow players to own unique assets they purchase. Also, once a player owns an in-game asset NFT, they can freely sell it outside the platform where it was created, which is not possible for regular games. Players also have a say in the governance of the game itself. A few success metrics here include:

The number of active players – this involves assessing the number of daily and monthly active players of a game which shows a rise in popularity.

Transaction volume per user – you can use this metric to measure the average amount of funds transferred per player. It is indicative of the level of user engagement and the soundness of the token design.

Number and quality of guild partnerships – Most Web3 games will rely on player referrals and partnerships with guilds to achieve growth and wide distribution. Top guilds will allow new players to get started on a game by loaning them game assets that they might otherwise not be able to afford. They also help P2E games gain increase in daily active users through scholarships, online markets, and direct investments.

This is by no means an exhaustive list; however, it serves to make it easy for users to analyse the growth of a given protocol by applying the metrics above.

CHAPTER EIGHTEEN

The Future of Web3 Payment Systems

The Future of Web3 Payment Systems

The internet is going through a transformation, and Web3 is the new frontier. It is backed by blockchain applications that enable seamless transactions using cryptocurrencies, boosting frictionless global trade. This revolution is slowly making conventional fiat payment systems obsolete. It is no secret that international payments made through traditional solutions can take several days to clear. Blockchain payment solutions allow the process to take a few hours, if not minutes.

Over the years, traditional payment systems have suffered from long processing times, especially when it comes to cross-border payments. Some Web2 solutions, such as PayPal and Stripe, have improved the situation; however, they are not without limitations. For instance, a Web3 version of PayPal will not be able to freeze a user's account or withhold payment due to an expired proof of address. This is where blockchain solutions come in. They are taking it to the next level with much lower costs, reduced risk, and efficacy.

Blockchain is the Future

Top companies in the payment sector seem to understand that blockchain represents the next evolution within the industry. Over the past few years, they have been busy researching and exploring how to use the technology to their benefit. A good example is Mastercard and Visa, who have both partnered with crypto exchanges and wallets to facilitate crypto-related transactions. In the last quarter of 2021, crypto-related payments using Visa amounted to over 5% of all transactions processed by the payment giant. In April 2022, Mastercard announced the world's first crypto-backed credit card.

Despite these forays, both giants' core business models remain firmly rooted in Web2, with blockchain sitting as a side-line service. Much work needs to be done to facilitate the widespread acceptance of blockchain-based payment solutions around the world. More research, infrastructure investment, government regulations and directives will be required.

Along that line, a possible solution to developing a global public blockchain-based payment infrastructure could be to develop private blockchains for key players that need to transact with one another frequently. For instance, J.P. Morgan recently launched the Link blockchain specifically designed for financial organizations. In its current state, the blockchain enables an efficient and reliable exchange of information between its participants.

For now, no one knows what the future holds for Link; however, there is a chance that the platform or a future competitor could become a platform for instant and secure inter-bank payments, eventually evolving into a universal Web3 payment system. If this happens, then there can be no guarantee that the benefits realized by those within the "exclusive club" would be passed on to non-members, such as consumers. That said, the only challenge with private blockchains is their lack of transparency for financial institutions, whose reputations have already been tarnished by past scandals.

Other Industries Will Benifit

A private blockchain can also help many other industries such as insurance companies, airlines, and any other industry riddled by costs, friction, and anomalies when transacting with multiple counterparties. As products and trade become more complex, revenue and liability recognition are becoming more challenging for these industries. For instance, in the airline industry, the total revenue collected from the customer needs to be allocated to multiple parties based on nuanced code-sharing arrangements such as in-flight enhancements, seat selection fees, luggage upgrades, airport car parking, terminal throughput, etc.

Trying to work out pay-outs for all the parties involved, especially if there are delays or cancellations, can quickly descend into chaos, with final outcomes potentially reliant on judgment calls. Therefore, having all the players operating within the same blockchain can completely automate the process and, thanks to smart contracts, remove dependence on trust and erroneous errors.

As things stand, it seems like we are on the brink of the Web3 payment revolution. Given their enormous budgets and resources, it is entirely possible the revolution is going to be driven from the top, with initiators being Web2 or even Web1-based payment processing giants. At the same time, there is no ruling out a crypto-native startup reinventing the playing field instantly. And we are already witnessing the launch of several decentralized-based Web3 payment solutions that address the downside of centralization and offer a seamless payment experience.

These protocols are removing most of the barriers that currently stand in the way of mass adoption of Web3 payments, such as perceived ease of use, increase in the number of acceptable tokens, any-to-any conversion functionalities and so on. Businesses can benefit by integrating with such solutions as they help them accept any tokens or assets their customers hold in their wallets since most of them are interoperable, scalable and flexible.

CHAPTER NINETEEN

The Metaverse & Web3 - Blockchain

In recent years (2022), blockchain has gained widespread attention, followed by the meta-universe craze, and recently the discussion about Web3 has heated up again, with Tesla CEO Elon Musk, former Twitter CEO Jack Dorsey and various academics frequently bringing up the concept. So what exactly is the relationship between these technology buzzwords? What is the lineage of their development? And what is the ultimate form of Internet development?

With the continuous development of blockchain+ in the last few years, the concept of blockchain is no longer new to us. Blockchain is a decentralized data ledger that is securely shared. In a blockchain system, data cannot be changed without the permission of a prescribed number of people, which helps prevent fraud and data tampering. In other words, blockchain ledgers can be shared, but not altered. If one party tries to alter the data, all participants in the blockchain will be alerted as to which party is trying to do so.

Blockchain technology can thus be applied in a variety of ways across the enterprise, such as: providing reliable shared data and building trust between parties, eliminating data silos by integrating data into one system through a decentralized ledger, imbuing data of a high security degree with lesser need for third-party intermediaries, creating real-time, tamper-proof records shared among all participants, ensuring the authenticity and integrity of products in the flow of commerce, and seamlessly tracking goods and services throughout the supply chain.

Blockchain has expanded from banking to distributed applications in multiple verticals, including communications, media and manufacturing. Companies that rely on centralized control of user identities may find their business models challenged by blockchain.

Other tech buzzwords that are gradually coming into the limelight are Web3 and meta-universe. What is the relationship of these three concepts? Goldman Sachs described in a research report that blockchain technology is at the heart of the development of meta-universe and Web3.0.

Web 3 is a concept related to Web 1 and Web 2. The early Internet is known as Web 1, which was a readable network, where the website owners had great rights. But many individual websites were heavily scattered and content was duplicated, making it unsuccessful in attracting new users.

The Web 2 stage is a readable and writable Internet, which saw the emergence of UGC, i.e. user-generated content. Typical Web 2.0 sites include online communities, web applications, social networking sites, blogs, wikis, etc.

Web 3 is a more humane Internet, incorporating newer technologies, big data, artificial intelligence, etc. In the view of blockchain practitioners, Web 3 is the Internet that users can own, sometimes partially. There are four features of Web 3: unified identity authentication system, data authorization, privacy protection and anti-censorship, and decentralized operation. The core feature of Web 3 is that users are in charge of their own data. In a word, Web 3 is actually a new network form evolved based on blockchain thinking. A more mature case is the Ethernet and the decentralized applications built on it. Of course, the proportion of Web 3.0 still takes up a small proportion in the Internet world, but this model against the monopoly will be widely accepted, as its network form is presented in a decentralized way.

The decentralized network based on Web3 has also given rise to decentralized autonomous organizations (DAOs) of its match, which are driven by the creators themselves. By far only a small portion of DAOs are maturely developed.

Through the blockchain-based network, a new digital world driven by co-creative, co-built, and shared creators has begun to emerge. Therefore, the metaverse world is the applicational scenario of Web3.

The evolution of blockchain, artificial intelligence, digital twins, human-computer interaction, Internet of Things and other data-oriented information technologies is not happening by chance, but as technical preparation for the evolution from Web 2 to Web 3. From the technical point of view, metaverse is a credible digital network of value interaction, which is based on the support of Web3 technology system and operation mechanism, and a digital ecosystem with blockchain as the core. In the future, a large number of innovative business models in the digital environment will arise and form a new paradigm in the digital space.

Blockchain is just one of the many technologies among the metaverse concepts. The metaverse is an immersive digital world created by a fusion of virtual reality, augmented reality and the Internet. The connotations and key technologies of the metaverse require immersion, delivery of value, and further breakthrough of the spatial and temporal limitation.

Not all are in favor of Web 3 and the metaverse, whose development is still in the early stage with controversy. The internet industry is required to understand correctly how the development of technology is to guide the way for the Internet.

As the successor of Internet, metaverse may become the new direction of Internet development and the next stage of digital economy, among which are 5G, artificial intelligence, blockchain, cloud computing and big data, and also in corporation with the VR, AR, brain-computer interface, Internet of Things and other technologies. The exploration of metaverse will promote a deep integration of real and digital world, for the door between virtual and real has been open.

CHAPTER TWENTY

A Complete Guide to The Web3 Stack

There are a lot of different definitions surrounding Web3, which fundamentally represents a set of technologies that is making the web more interactive. From a crypto perspective, Web3 represents a trustless, permissionless, decentralized internet that leverages distributed ledger technology. The outstanding feature of Web3 is ownership. While the first iteration of the commercial internet (Web1) was read-only for most users, the advent of Web2 allowed users to read and write on centralized platforms such as Facebook, Twitter, YouTube, etc. Right now, Web3 gives users full ownership over their content, data, and assets. Simply put, it empowers users to read, write and own their creations.

While third parties like Facebook get to own your identity and data in Web2, your identity in Web3 moves fluidly between platforms without your data being captured and monetized by service providers. Given that Web2 apps are centrally controlled, tokens in Web3 grant users the right to help govern the services they use, representing a form of ownership in the platforms themselves. With this in mind, what does the Web3 stack look like?

The Web 3 Stack

These are the early days of Web3, and for this reason, it is still much fragmented, albeit with much innovation over the past few years. This is not a completely exhaustive outline of what Web3 is supposed to be; instead, it is a framework to refine this landscape as it continues to evolve. Let us cover the four main layers, starting from the bottom up.

Protocol Layer

This is the bottom layer made up of the underlying blockchain architecture on top of which everything else gets built. Bitcoin paved the way, and even though it does not play a major role in Web3 today, the protocol made it possible for anyone to own a scarce digital asset through the use of public-private key cryptography.

After Bitcoin came several layer 1 smart contract platforms such as Ethereum, Solana, Avalanche, Cosmos, etc., that serve as the foundation for many Web3 applications in production today. Both Bitcoin and Ethereum have additional protocols built on top of them. In Bitcoin's case, Lightning Network facilitates fast and cheap payments. In Ethereum's case, a few layer-2 scaling protocols have been built to help address its underlying issues.

The rise of layer 1 and layer 2 networks brought about the need to bridge value between them. This is where cross-chain bridges that serve as highways come in, allowing users to move value from one chain to another.

Infrastructure / Category Primitives

This layer sits on top of the protocol layer, and is composed of interoperable building blocks known as "category primitives" that are highly reliable at doing a specific task. This is a dense and diverse layer where projects are building everything - smart contract auditing software, data storage, communication protocols, data analytics platforms, DAO governance tooling, identity solutions, financial primitives, and more.

A few good examples here include Uniswap, a protocol that allows the swapping of one asset for another, and Arweave, which enables data to be stored in a decentralized manner. The point is a user cannot do much with the standalone application, but when combined, these category primitives serve as Lego bricks that a Web3 developer can use to construct an app.

Use Case Layer

This is where it all comes together. For example, Axie Infinity uses Ethereum tokens and NFTs that can be bridged to a low-cost/ high throughput sidechain called Ronin. Players use DEXs such as Uniswap to swap ETH for the tokens needed to play the game. Another good example is Mirror, a decentralized blogging platform that uses Arweave, a storage protocol to store data. Meanwhile, the protocol leverages Ethereum to let publishers get paid in crypto, often by directing tokens to their ENS address. If you have noticed, Uniswap appears both in our infrastructure and use case sections, but do not let this confuse you. Even though Uniswap is simply a series of smart contracts at its core, it also provides a frontend that users can interact with directly. In simple terms, it simultaneously serves as a standalone user-facing app and infrastructure for other Web3 apps like Axie Infinity.

Access Layer

At the top is the access layer hosting apps that serve as the entry point for all manner of Web3 activities. So, do you want to play Axie Infinity, or get paid for your content on Mirror? You will first need a wallet that serves as the main point of entry for most Web3 apps. You can employ the services of fiat on-ramps such as Moonpay, Wyre, or exchanges such as Binance and Coinbase that help you to trade your fiat for crypto to get started. Once you have crypto in your wallet, you can head to an aggregator such as DappRadar to browse through and connect to all kinds of Web3 apps in one place.

Remember, the protocols, infrastructure, user applications, and access points named above make up the nascent yet evolving world of Web3, an internet that its users own. Beyond ownership, the power of Web3 lies in its modularity and interoperability. Therefore, there are endless ways that the above stack can be combined to create new and exciting use cases.

CHAPTER TWENTY-ONE

CAREER OPPORTUNITIES IN WEB 3.0

How to Start A Career in Web 3.0

Web 3.0 is expected to be a gamechanger that impacts various aspects of our lives, such as how we trade, communicate and trust. Lately, there has been a lot of buzz surrounding it, thanks to NFTs, metaverse and other innovations around the blockchain industry. Thanks to its underlying principles and technology, a lot of money is being put into the development of Web 3.0 solutions, and this has seen more people contemplating a career in Web 3.0. If you are such an individual, then you should read on. This piece will offer a few tips on how you can get started in this new field.

Shifting from Web 2.0 to Web 3.0

Do not let the terminology scare you. Web 2.0 is a term used to describe the internet as you know it today. It consists of social media sites, blogs, and online communities that allow end-users to interact and collaborate in real-time. The web relies on intermediaries and is dominated by companies that provide services in exchange for your data. That said, this web is flawed in many ways. To address issues around the web, another version of it is on the rise.

Web 3.0 brings about a decentralized internet, where third parties have less control over user interaction and value transfers. Essentially, this web is laying the foundation for P2P communication, payments, services and marketplaces. At the same time, blockchain technology is playing a vital role in shaping the development of Web 3.0.

Therefore, it is vital to understand how blockchain works if you intend to start a career in Web 3.0. If you have worked in tech, you may already have most of the required skills. Let us go over a few steps that someone with zero knowledge of blockchain technology should take.

Start Learning About Web 3.0

Starting a career in this new web is no different from starting one in any other industry. The first steps involve learning the basics, such as reading the news. It will also help if you understand what blockchain is all about, and how it works.

There are plenty of free resources to help out if you are willing to dedicate some time. Apart from the many videos, online courses and other resources such as Binance Academy that you can find online, follow the major news sites such as Cointelegraph and CoinDesk to stay updated on the latest happenings within the industry.

Others skill needed

The next step is getting more technical to become an expert on the subject. This involves understanding various tech stacks needed to create a given product. Also, you can read the likes of 'Mastering Bitcoin and Mastering Ethereum' by Andreas Antonopoulos. Also, we would recommend that you read a few whitepapers belonging to major projects, such as Bitcoin, Ethereum, Cardano, Polkadot, Solana, Decentraland, etc.

Career Opportunities in Web 3.0

If you decide to enter this new industry, you can pursue various careers. Below are a few notable ones.

Blockchain Core Devloper

As a blockchain core developer, you will be responsible for building blockchain architecture, designing protocols and consensus mechanism, and making and implementing high-level decisions related to the blockchain network. Therefore, you need to be familiar and experienced with Blockchain architecture, cryptographic hash functions, consensus mechanisms, algorithms, distributed ledger technology, and various data structures such as Merkle Trees, Patricia Trees etc., some of the languages you will be using include Golang, Rust, C++, and Java.

You can also opt to be a **blockchain software developer**, or **blockchain dApp developer**. As the name says, this role involves building decentralized applications on top of blockchains. Here, you need to be experienced in various development tools and languages such as Solidity or Substrate.

Then there is the **front-end developer** where you will be building beautiful and functional user interfaces and writing well-tested and reliable code. This means you will be working closely with UX/UI designers to deliver the best experience to the end-user.

DevOps Engineers are in charge of facilitating seamless delivery of high-quality products and updates to end-users, and doing it fast. You will help coders do their work best by ensuring the correct code gets to the right place. You will also deal with infrastructure maintenance, monitoring, process automation, building and delivering software from GitHub to serves.

As for places you can look to start your career, you can consider blockchain infrastructure development companies, start-ups, consulting companies, big tech, and the financial sector. Also, consider using websites such as Glassdoor, CryptocurrencyJobs, CryptoJobs, Upwork, CryptoCareers and so on to identify suitable jobs that match your skills. Finally, you can consider applying for bounties and hackathons at Gitcoin.

Blockchain

1.
Blockchain Technology

2. SMART CONTRACT
3.
Cryptocurrency

4.
NFT

CHAPTER TWENTY-TWO

BLOCKCHAIN TECHNOLOGY

What Is Blockchain Technology?

Blockchain is a list of records called blocks that store data publicly and in chronological order. The information is encrypted using cryptography to ensure that the privacy of the user is not compromised and data cannot be altered.

Blockchain is a method of recording information that makes it impossible or difficult for the system to be changed, hacked, or manipulated. A blockchain is a distributed ledger that duplicates and distributes transactions across the network of computers participating in the blockchain.

Blockchain technology is a structure that stores transactional records, also known as the block, of the public in several databases, known as the "chain," in a network connected through peer-to-peer nodes. Typically, this storage is referred to as a 'digital ledger.'

Every transaction in this ledger is authorized by the digital signature of the owner, which authenticates the transaction and safeguards it from tampering. Hence, the information the digital ledger contains is highly secure.

In simpler words, the digital ledger is like a Google spreadsheet shared among numerous computers in a network, in which, the transactional records are stored based on actual purchases. The fascinating angle is that anybody can see the data, but they can't corrupt it.

Information on a Blockchain network is not controlled by a centralized authority, unlike modern financial institutions. The participants of the network maintain the data, and they hold the democratic authority to approve any transaction which can happen on a Blockchain network. Therefore, a typical Blockchain network is a public Blockchain.

As long as you have access to the network, you have access to the data within the Blockchain. If you are a participant in the Blockchain network, you will have the same copy of the ledger, which all other participants have. Even if one node or data on one particular participant computer gets corrupted, the other participants will be alerted immediately, and they can rectify it as soon as possible.

History of Blockchain

In 1982, David Chaum proposed the first-ever blockchain-like protocol in his dissertation, Computer Systems Established, Maintained, and Trusted by Mutually Suspicious Groups. This concept was further worked on by Stuart Haber and W Scott Stornetta in 1991, where they described the process of a cryptographically secured chain of blocks with timestamps that could not be tampered with.

Satoshi Nakamoto, first introduced the concept of blockchains in 2008. The design continued to improve and evolve, with Nakamoto using a Hashcash-like method. It eventually became a primary component of bitcoin, a popular form of cryptocurrency, where it serves as a public ledger for all network transactions.

Bitcoin blockchain file sizes, which contained all transactions and records on the network, continued to grow substantially. By August 2014, it had reached 20 gigabytes, and eventually exceeded 400 gigabytes by July 2022.

Why is Blockchain Popular?

Suppose you are transferring money to your family or friends from your bank account. You would log in to online banking and transfer the amount to the other person using their account number. When the transaction is done, your bank updates the transaction records. It seems simple enough, right? There is a potential issue which most of us neglect.

These types of transactions can be tampered with very quickly. People who are familiar with this truth are often wary of using these types of transactions, hence the evolution of third-party payment applications in recent years. But this vulnerability is essentially why Blockchain technology was created.

Technologically, Blockchain is a digital ledger that is gaining a lot of attention and traction recently. But why has it become so popular? Well, let's dig into it to fathom the whole concept.

Record keeping of data and transactions are a crucial part of the business. Often, this information is handled in house or passed through a third party like brokers, bankers, or lawyers increasing time, cost, or both on the business. Fortunately, Blockchain avoids this long process and facilitates the faster movement of the transaction, thereby saving both time and money.

Most people assume Blockchain and Bitcoin can be used interchangeably, but in reality, that's not the case. Blockchain is the technology capable of supporting various applications related to multiple industries like finance, supply chain, manufacturing, etc., but Bitcoin is a currency that relies on Blockchain technology to be secure.

Blockchain is an emerging technology with many advantages in an increasingly digital world:

Highly Secure

It uses a digital signature feature to conduct fraud-free transactions making it impossible to corrupt or change the data of an individual by the other users without a specific digital signature.

Decentralized System

Conventionally, you need the approval of regulatory authorities like a government or bank for transactions; however, with Blockchain, transactions are done with the mutual consensus of users resulting in smoother, safer, and faster transactions.

Automation Capability

It is programmable and can generate systematic actions, events, and payments automatically when the criteria of the trigger are met.

How Does Blockchain Technology Work?

In recent years, you may have noticed many businesses around the world integrating Blockchain technology. But how exactly does Blockchain technology work? Is this a significant change or a simple addition? The advancements of Blockchain are still young and have the potential to be revolutionary in the future; so, let's begin demystifying this technology.

Blockchain is a combination of three leading technologies:

1. Cryptographic keys
2. A peer-to-peer network containing a shared ledger
3. A means of computing, to store the transactions and records of the network

Cryptography keys consist of two keys – Private key and Public key. These keys help in performing successful transactions between two parties. Each individual has these two keys, which they use to produce a secure digital identity reference. This secured identity is the most important aspect of Blockchain technology. In the world of cryptocurrency, this identity is referred to as 'digital signature' and is used for authorizing and controlling transactions.

The digital signature is merged with the peer-to-peer network; a large number of individuals who act as authorities use the digital signature in order to reach a consensus on transactions, among other issues. When they authorize a deal, it is certified by a mathematical verification, which results in a successful secured transaction between the two network-connected parties. So to sum it up, Blockchain users employ cryptography keys to perform different types of digital interactions over the peer-to-peer network.

Types of Blockchain Networks

There are several ways to build a blockchain network. They can be public, private, permissioned or built by a consortium.

Public blockchain networks

A public blockchain is one that anyone can join and participate in, such as Bitcoin. Drawbacks might include substantial computational power required, little or no privacy for transactions, and weak security. These are important considerations for enterprise use cases of blockchain.

Private Blockchain Networks

A private blockchain network, similar to a public blockchain network, is a decentralized peer-to-peer network. However, one organization governs the network, controlling who is allowed to participate, execute a consensus protocol and maintain the shared ledger. Depending on the use case, this can significantly boost trust and confidence between participants. A private blockchain can be run behind a corporate firewall and even be hosted on premises.

Permissioned Blockchain Networks

Businesses who set up a private blockchain will generally set up a permissioned blockchain network. It is important to note that public blockchain networks can also be permissioned. This places restrictions on who is allowed to participate in the network and in what transactions. Participants need to obtain an invitation or permission to join.

Consortium Blockchains

Multiple organizations can share the responsibilities of maintaining a blockchain. These pre-selected organizations determine who may submit transactions or access the data. A consortium blockchain is ideal for business when all participants need to be permissioned and have a shared responsibility for the blockchain.

The Process of Transaction

One of Blockchain technology's cardinal features is the way it confirms and authorizes transactions. For example, if two individuals wish to perform a transaction with a private and public key, respectively, the first person party would attach the transaction information to the public key of the second party. This total information is gathered together into a block.

The block contains a digital signature, a timestamp, and other important, relevant information. It should be noted that the block doesn't include the identities of the individuals involved in the transaction. This block is then transmitted across all of the network's nodes, and when the right individual uses his private key and matches it with the block, the transaction gets completed successfully.

In addition to conducting financial transactions, the Blockchain can also hold transactional details of properties, vehicles, etc.

Here's a use case that illustrates how Blockchain works:

•

Hash Encryptions

blockchain technology uses hashing and encryption to secure the data, relying mainly on the SHA256 algorithm to secure the information. The address of the sender (public key), the receiver's address, the transaction, and his/her private key details are transmitted via the SHA256 algorithm. The encrypted information, called hash encryption, is transmitted across the world and added to the blockchain after verification. The SHA256 algorithm makes it almost impossible to hack the hash encryption, which in turn simplifies the sender and receiver's authentication.

-

Proof of Work

In a Blockchain, each block consists of 4 main headers.

- Previous Hash: This hash address locates the previous block.
- Transaction Details: Details of all the transactions that need to occur.
- Nonce: An arbitrary number given in cryptography to differentiate the block's hash address.
- Hash Address of the Block: All of the above (i.e., preceding hash, transaction details, and nonce) are transmitted through a hashing algorithm. This gives an output containing a 256-bit, 64 character length value, which is called the unique 'hash address.' Consequently, it is referred to as the hash of the block.
- Numerous people around the world try to figure out the right hash value to meet a pre-determined condition using computational algorithms. The transaction completes when the predetermined condition is met. To put it more plainly, Blockchain miners attempt to solve a mathematical puzzle, which is referred to as a proof of work problem. Whoever solves it first gets a reward.

Mining

In Blockchain technology, the process of adding transactional details to the present digital/public ledger is called 'mining.' Though the term is associated with Bitcoin, it is used to refer to other Blockchain technologies as well. Mining involves generating the hash of a block transaction, which is tough to forge, thereby ensuring the safety of the entire Blockchain without needing a central system.

Advantages and Disadvantages of Blockchain

Like all forms of technology, blockchain has several advantages and disadvantages to consider.

Advantages

One major advantage of blockchains is the level of security it can provide, and this also means that blockchains can protect and secure sensitive data from online transactions. For anyone looking for speedy and convenient transactions, blockchain technology offers this as well. In fact, it only takes a few minutes, whereas other transaction methods can take several days to complete. There is also no third-party interference from financial institutions or government organizations, which many users look at as an advantage.

Disadvantages

Blockchain and cryptography involves the use of public and private keys, and reportedly, there have been problems with private keys. If a user loses their private key, they face numerous challenges, making this one disadvantage of blockchains. Another disadvantage is the scalability restrictions, as the number of transactions per node is limited. Because of this, it can take several hours to finish multiple transactions and other tasks. It can also be difficult to change or add information after it is recorded, which is another significant disadvantage of blockchain.

How to Invest in Blockchain Technology

Blockchain technology and stocks can be a lucrative investment, and there are several ways to take the next step toward making your first blockchain investment purchase. Bitcoin is typically the first thing that comes to mind when it comes to investing in blockchain technology, and it shouldn't be overlooked. Aside from Bitcoin, there is also the option of investing in cryptocurrency penny stocks, such as Altcoin and Litecoin. There are also certain apps and services that are in the pre-development phase and that are using blockchain technology to raise funding. As an investor, you can buy coins, with the expectation that prices will go up if the service or app becomes popular. Another way to invest in blockchain technology is to invest in startups built on blockchain technology. Finally, there is always the option to invest in pure blockchain technology.

Uses of Blockchain

The use of blockchain goes far beyond cryptocurrency and bitcoin. Here are some of the most common uses of blockchain in different industries:

- Anti-money laundering tracking system
- NFT marketplaces
- Original content creation
- Real-time IoT operating systems
- Advertising insights
- Music royalties tracking
- Cross-border payments
- Voting mechanism

- Supply chain and logistics monitoring

How Will Blockchain Disrupt Industries?

Several industries like Unilever, Walmart, Visa, etc. use blockchain technology and have gained benefits in transparency, security, and traceability. Considering the benefits blockchain offers, it will revolutionize and redefine many sectors.

Here are the top 5 prominent industries that will be disrupted by blockchain technology in the near future:

1.Banking
2.Cyber Security
3.Supply Chain Management
4.Healthcare
5.Government

1. Banking

Before Blockchain

Banking has transfer fees, which can be both expensive and time-consuming for people. Also, sending money overseas becomes even more difficult due to the exchange rate and other hidden costs.

After Blockchain

Blockchain eliminates the need for a middleman. Blockchain is disrupting the banking system by providing a peer-to-peer payment system with the highest security and low fees.

- Blockchain technology provides instant and borderless payments across the globe
- Cryptocurrencies (like Ethereum, bitcoin) remove the requirement for a third party to perform transactions
- Blockchain records all the transactions in a public ledger which is globally accessible by bitcoin users

Let's consider an example of ABRA

Abra is a financial cryptocurrency application which helps in performing peer-to-peer money transfers

With this application, cryptocurrency users can save, send and receive their digital money on their electronic devices

2. Cyber Security

Before Blockchain

Earlier, cyberattacks were a significant threat to the public. Several organizations were developing an effective solution to secure the data against unauthorized access and tampering.

After Blockchain

- Blockchain quickly identifies malicious attack due to the peer-to-peer connections where data cannot be tampered with
- Every single piece of data stored on the blockchain network is verified and encrypted using a cryptographic algorithm
- By eliminating the centralized system, blockchain provides a transparent and secure way of recording transactions (without disclosing your private information to anyone)

For example, a software security company called Guardtime offers blockchain-based products and services.

Rather than following the centralized system, the company utilizes blockchain technology and distributes data to its nodes.

3. Supply Chain Management

Before Blockchain

Due to the lack of transparency, supply chain management often had its challenges like service redundancy, lack of coordination between various departments, and lack of reliability.

After Blockchain

Tracking of a product can be done with blockchain technology, by facilitating traceability across the entire Supply chain.

Blockchain gives the facility to verify and audit transactions by multiple supply chain partners involved in the supply chain management system.

- Blockchain records transaction (history, timestamp, date, etc.) of a product in a decentralized distributed ledger
- Each transaction is recorded into a block
- With blockchain, anyone can verify the authenticity or status of a product being delivered

Let's consider an example of the Pacific Tuna project.

Here, blockchain supply chain management provides a step-by-step verification process to track tuna fish. The process results in preventing illegal fishing.

4. Healthcare

Before Blockchain

In the healthcare system, patients can connect to other hospitals and collect their medical data immediately. Apart from the delay, there are high data corruption chances since the information is stored in a physical memory system.

After Blockchain

- Blockchain removes a central authority, which results in instant access to data
- Here, each block is linked to another block and distributed across the computer node. This becomes difficult for a hacker to corrupt the data

For example, United Healthcare is an American healthcare company that has enhanced its privacy, security, and medical records' interoperability using Blockchain.

5. Government

Before Blockchain

Rigged votes is an illegal activity that occurs during most traditional voting systems. Also, citizens who want to vote to wait a little longer in a queue and cast their votes to a local authority, which is a very time-consuming process.

After Blockchain

- Voters are allowed to vote without the need of disclosing their identity in public
- The votes are counted with high accuracy by the officials knowing that each ID can be attributed to just one vote
- As soon the vote is added to the public ledger, the information can never be erased

Consider an example of MiVote

- MiVote is a token-based blockchain platform that is similar to a digital ballot box
- Using MiVote, through a smartphone, voters can cast their votes, where the records are stored in the blockchain securely

Moving forward, let's understand the fundamentals of Blockchain.

CHAPTER TWENTY-THREE

WHAT IS A SMART CONTRACT IN BLOCKCHAIN ?

What Is Smart Contract?

Smart contracts are computer programs or protocols for automated transactions that are stored on a blockchain and run in response to meeting certain conditions. In other words, smart contracts automate the execution of agreements so that all participants can ascertain the outcome as soon as possible without the involvement of an intermediary or time delay.

- Smart contracts are self-executing contracts in which the contents of the buyer-seller agreement are inscribed directly into lines of code.
- According to Nick Szabo, an American computer scientist who devised a virtual currency called "Bit Gold" in 1998, Smart contracts are computerized transaction protocols that execute contract conditions.
- Using it makes the transactions traceable, transparent, and irreversible.

Benefits of Smart Contracts

Accuracy, Speed, and Efficiency

- The contract is immediately executed when a condition is met.
- Because smart contracts are digital and automated, there is no paperwork to deal with, and
- No time was spent correcting errors that can occur when filling out documentation by hand.

Trust and Transparency

- There's no need to worry about information being tampered with for personal gain because there's no third party engaged and
- Encrypted transaction logs are exchanged among participants.

Security

- Because blockchain transaction records are encrypted, they are extremely difficult to hack.
- Furthermore, because each entry on a distributed ledger is linked to the entries before and after it, hackers would have to change the entire chain to change a single record.

Savings

- Smart contracts eliminate the need for intermediaries to conduct transactions, as well as the time delays and fees that come with them

How Do Smart Contracts Work?

A smart contract is a sort of program that encodes business logic and operates on a dedicated virtual machine embedded in a blockchain or other distributed ledger.

Step 1: Business teams collaborate with developers to define their criteria for the smart contract's desired behavior in response to certain events or circumstances.

Step 2: Conditions such as payment authorization, shipment receipt, or a utility meter reading threshold are examples of simple events.

Step 3: More complex operations, such as determining the value of a derivative financial instrument, or automatically releasing an insurance payment, might be encoded using more sophisticated logic.

Step 4: The developers then use a smart contract writing platform to create and test the logic. After the application is written, it is sent to a separate team for security testing.

Step 5: An internal expert or a company that specializes in vetting smart contract security could be used.

Step 6: The contract is then deployed on an existing blockchain or other distributed ledger infrastructure once it has been authorized.

Step 7: The smart contract is configured to listen for event updates from an "oracle," which is effectively a cryptographically secure streaming data source, once it has been deployed.

Step 8: Once it obtains the necessary combination of events from one or more oracles, the smart contract executes

Blockchain Implementation of a Smart Contract and Crowdfunding

Ethereum-based smart contracts may be used to create digital tokens for performing transactions. You may design and issue your own digital currency, creating a tradable computerized token. The tokens use a standard coin API. In the case of Ethereum, there are standardizations of ERC 2.0, allowing the contract to access any wallet for exchange automatically. As a result, you build a tradable token with a fixed supply. The platform becomes a central bank of sorts, issuing digital money.

Suppose you want to start a business requiring funding. But who would lend money to someone they don't know or trust? Smart contracts have a major role to play. With Ethereum, you can build a smart contract to hold a contributor's funds until a given date passes or a goal is met. Based on the result, the funds are released to the contract owners or sent back to the contributors. The centralized crowdfunding system has many issues with management systems. To combat this, a DAO (Decentralized Autonomous Organization) is utilized for crowdfunding. The terms and conditions are set in the contract, and every individual participating in crowdfunding is given a token. Every contribution is recorded on the Blockchain.

Voting and Blockchain Implementation of Smart Contracts

Using Blockchain in the voting process can eliminate common problems. A centralized voting system faces difficulties when it comes to tracking votes – identity fraud, miscounts, or bias by voting officials. Using a smart contract, certain predefined terms and conditions are pre-set in the contract. No voter can vote from a digital identity other than his or her own. The counting is foolproof. Every vote is registered on a blockchain network, and the counting is tallied automatically with no interference from a third party or dependency on a manual process. Each ID is attributed to just one vote. Validation is accomplished by the users on the blockchain network itself. Thus, the voting process can be in a public blockchain, or it could be in a decentralized autonomous organization-based blockchain setup. As a result, every vote is recorded on the ledger, and the information cannot be modified. That ledger is publicly available for audit and verification.

Smart contracts allow you to create voting systems in which you can add and remove members, change voting rules, change debating periods, or alter the majority rule. For instance, you can create a vote for a decision within a decentralized autonomous organization. Rather than a central authority making a decision, a voting mechanism within the organization can determine whether the proposal is accepted or rejected.

Limitation of Smart Contracts

- Because smart contracts can't send HTTP queries, they can't acquire information about "real-world" events. This is by design.
- Using external data could jeopardize consensus, which is critical for security and decentralization.

Use Cases of Smart Contracts

- The use cases for smart contracts range from simple to complex.
- They can be used for simple economic transactions, such as moving money from point A to point B, as well as for smart access management in the sharing economy.
- Smart contracts could disrupt many industries.
- Banking, insurance, energy, e-government, telecommunications, the music business, art, mobility, education, and many other industries have use cases.

CHAPTER TWENTY-FOUR

WHAT IS CRYPTOCURRENCY?

A Brief History of Cryptocurrency

In the caveman era, people used the barter system, in which goods and services are exchanged among two or more people. For instance, someone might exchange seven apples for seven oranges. The barter system fell out of popular use because it had some glaring flaws:

- People's requirements have to coincide—if you have something to trade, someone else has to want it, and you have to want what the other person is offering.
- There's no common measure of value—you have to decide how many of your items you are willing to trade for other items, and not all items can be divided. For example, you cannot divide a live animal into smaller units.
- The goods cannot be transported easily, unlike our modern currency, which fits in a wallet or is stored on a mobile phone.

After people realized the barter system didn't work very well, the currency went through a few iterations: In 110 B.C., an official currency was minted; in A.D. 1250, gold-plated florins were introduced and used across Europe; and from 1600 to 1900, the paper currency gained widespread popularity and ended up being used around the world. This is how modern currency as we know it came into existence.

Modern currency includes paper currency, coins, credit cards, and digital wallets—for example, Apple Pay, Amazon Pay, Paytm, PayPal, and so on. All of it is controlled by banks and governments, meaning that there is a centralized regulatory authority that limits how paper currency and credit cards work.

Traditional Currencies vs. Cryptocurrencies

Imagine a scenario in which you want to repay a friend who bought you lunch, by sending money online to his or her account. There are several ways in which this could go wrong, including:

- The financial institution could have a technical issue, such as its systems are down or the machines aren't working properly.
- Your or your friend's account could have been hacked—for example, there could be a denial-of-service attack or identity theft.
- The transfer limits for your or your friend's account could have been exceeded.

What is Cryptocurrency?

A cryptocurrency is a coded string of data representing a currency unit. Peer-to-peer networks called blockchains monitor and organize cryptocurrency transactions, such as buying, selling, and transferring, and also serve as secure ledgers of transactions. By utilizing encryption technology, cryptocurrencies can serve as both a currency and an accounting system.

A cryptocurrency is a digital or virtual currency that is meant to be a medium of exchange. It is quite similar to real-world currency, except it does not have any physical embodiment, and it uses cryptography to work.

Because cryptocurrencies operate independently and in a decentralized manner, without a bank or a central authority, new units can be added only after certain conditions are met. For example, with Bitcoin, only after a block has been added to the blockchain will the miner be rewarded with bitcoins, and this is the only way new bitcoins can be generated. The limit for bitcoins is 21 million; after this, no more bitcoins will be produced

Benefits of Cryptocurrency

With cryptocurrency, the transaction cost is low to nothing at all—unlike, for example, the fee for transferring money from a digital wallet to a bank account. You can make transactions at any time of the day or night, and there are no limits on purchases and withdrawals. And anyone is free to use cryptocurrency, unlike setting up a bank account, which requires documentation and other paperwork.

International cryptocurrency transactions are faster than wire transfers too. Wire transfers take about half a day for the money to be moved from one place to another. With cryptocurrencies, transactions take only a matter of minutes or even seconds.

What is Cryptography?

Cryptography is a method of using encryption and decryption to secure communication in the presence of third parties with ill intent—that is, third parties who want to steal your data or eavesdrop on your conversation. Cryptography uses computational algorithms such as SHA-256, which is the hashing algorithm that Bitcoin uses; a public key, which is like a digital identity of the user shared with everyone; and a private key, which is a digital signature of the user that is kept hidden.

What Is Cryptocurrency: Types, Benefits, History and More

Lesson 4 of 31By Shivam Arora

Last updated on Sep 23, 202233961684

PreviousNext

Table of Contents

Cryptocurrencies have become increasingly popular over the past several years - as of 2018, there were more than 1,600 of them! And the number is constantly growing. With that has come to an increase in demand for developers of the blockchain (the underlying technology of cryptocurrencies such as bitcoin). The salaries blockchain developers earn show how much they are valued: According to Indeed, the average salary of a full-stack developer is more than $112,000. There's even a dedicated website for cryptocurrency jobs.

Whether you're interested in a career as a blockchain developer or you just want to keep up with the latest trends in tech, Simplilearn's Cryptocurrency Explained video explains what cryptocurrency is and why it's important will get you off to a good start. Here we'll recap what's covered in the video.

Caltech Blockchain Bootcamp

Learn how to set up private Blockchain networks.ENROLL NOW

A Brief History of Cryptocurrency

In the caveman era, people used the barter system, in which goods and services are exchanged among two or more people. For instance, someone might exchange seven apples for seven oranges. The barter system fell out of popular use because it had some glaring flaws:

People's requirements have to coincide—if you have something to trade, someone else has to want it, and you have to want what the other person is offering.

There's no common measure of value—you have to decide how many of your items you are willing to trade for other items, and not all items can be divided. For example, you cannot divide a live animal into smaller units.

The goods cannot be transported easily, unlike our modern currency, which fits in a wallet or is stored on a mobile phone.

After people realized the barter system didn't work very well, the currency went through a few iterations: In 110 B.C., an official currency was minted; in A.D. 1250, gold-plated florins were introduced and used across Europe; and from 1600 to 1900, the paper currency gained widespread popularity and ended up being used around the world. This is how modern currency as we know it came into existence.

Modern currency includes paper currency, coins, credit cards, and digital wallets—for example, Apple Pay, Amazon Pay, Paytm, PayPal, and so on. All of it is controlled by banks and governments, meaning that there is a centralized regulatory authority that limits how paper currency and credit cards work.

Traditional Currencies vs. Cryptocurrencies

Imagine a scenario in which you want to repay a friend who bought you lunch, by sending money online to his or her account. There are several ways in which this could go wrong, including:

The financial institution could have a technical issue, such as its systems are down or the machines aren't working properly.

Your or your friend's account could have been hacked—for example, there could be a denial-of-service attack or identity theft.

The transfer limits for your or your friend's account could have been exceeded.

There is a central point of failure: the bank.

This is why the future of currency lies with cryptocurrency. Now imagine a similar transaction between two people using the bitcoin app. A notification appears asking whether the person is sure he or she is ready to transfer bitcoins. If yes, processing takes place: The system authenticates the user's identity, checks whether the user has the required balance to make that transaction, and so on. After that's done, the payment is transferred and the money lands in the receiver's account. All of this happens in a matter of minutes.

Cryptocurrency, then, removes all the problems of modern banking: There are no limits to the funds you can transfer, your accounts cannot be hacked, and there is no central point of failure. As mentioned above, as of 2018 there are more than 1,600 cryptocurrencies available; some popular ones are Bitcoin, Litecoin, Ethereum, and Zcash. And a new cryptocurrency crops up every single day. Considering how much growth they're experiencing at the moment, there's a good chance that there are plenty more to come!

Moving forward, let us discuss what is cryptocurrency.

What is Cryptocurrency?

A cryptocurrency is a coded string of data representing a currency unit. Peer-to-peer networks called blockchains monitor and organize cryptocurrency transactions, such as buying, selling, and transferring, and also serve as secure ledgers of transactions. By utilizing encryption technology, cryptocurrencies can serve as both a currency and an accounting system.

A cryptocurrency is a digital or virtual currency that is meant to be a medium of exchange. It is quite similar to real-world currency, except it does not have any physical embodiment, and it uses cryptography to work.

Because cryptocurrencies operate independently and in a decentralized manner, without a bank or a central authority, new units can be added only after certain conditions are met. For example, with Bitcoin, only after a block has been added to the blockchain will the miner be rewarded with bitcoins, and this is the only way new bitcoins can be generated. The limit for bitcoins is 21 million; after this, no more bitcoins will be produced.

Benefits of Cryptocurrency

With cryptocurrency, the transaction cost is low to nothing at all—unlike, for example, the fee for transferring money from a digital wallet to a bank account. You can make transactions at any time of the day or night, and there are no limits on purchases and withdrawals. And anyone is free to use cryptocurrency, unlike setting up a bank account, which requires documentation and other paperwork.

Professional Certificate Program in Blockchain

in Collaboration with IIT KanpurENROLL NOW

International cryptocurrency transactions are faster than wire transfers too. Wire transfers take about half a day for the money to be moved from one place to another. With cryptocurrencies, transactions take only a matter of minutes or even seconds.

What is Cryptography?

Cryptography is a method of using encryption and decryption to secure communication in the presence of third parties with ill intent—that is, third parties who want to steal your data or eavesdrop on your conversation. Cryptography uses computational algorithms such as SHA-256, which is the hashing algorithm that Bitcoin uses; a public key, which is like a digital identity of the user shared with everyone; and a private key, which is a digital signature of the user that is kept hidden.

Attend masterclasses from experienced faculty and earn your prestigious IIT Kanpur certificate. Learn and get hands-on experience on the latest Blockchain platforms such as Ethereum & Hyperledger in our Professional Certificate Program in Blockchain in just 4 months!

Cryptography in Bitcoin Transactions

In a normal bitcoin transaction, first, there are the transaction details: whom you want to send the bitcoins to and how many bitcoins you want to send. Then the information is passed through a hashing algorithm. Bitcoin, as mentioned, uses the SHA-256 algorithm. The output is then passed through a signature algorithm with the user's private key, used to uniquely identify the user. The digitally signed output is then distributed across the network for other users to verify. This is done by using the sender's public key.

The users who check the transaction to see whether it's valid or not are known as miners. After this is done, the transaction and several others are added to the blockchain, where the details cannot be changed.

The Future of Cryptocurrency

The world is clearly divided when it comes to cryptocurrencies. On one side are supporters such as Bill Gates, Al Gore and Richard Branson, who say that cryptocurrencies are better than regular currencies. On the other side are people such as Warren Buffet, Paul Krugman, and Robert Shiller, who are against it. Krugman and Shiller, who are both Nobel Prize winners in the field of economics, call it a Ponzi scheme and a means for criminal activities.

In the future, there's going to be a conflict between regulation and anonymity. Since several cryptocurrencies have been linked with terrorist attacks, governments would want to regulate how cryptocurrencies work. On the other hand, the main emphasis of cryptocurrencies is to ensure that users remain anonymous.

Futurists believe that by the year 2030, cryptocurrencies will occupy 25 percent of national currencies, which means a significant chunk of the world would start believing in cryptocurrency as a mode of transaction. It's going to be increasingly accepted by merchants and customers, and it will continue to have a volatile nature, which means prices will continue to fluctuate, as they have been doing for the past few years.

CHAPTER TWENTY-FIVE

NFT

What is NFT?

NFT means non-fungible tokens (NFTs), which are generally created using the same type of programming used for cryptocurrencies. In simple terms these cryptographic assets are based on blockchain technology. They cannot be exchanged or traded equivalently like other cryptographic assets.

Like Bitcoin or Ethereum. The term NFT clearly represents it can neither be replaced nor interchanged because it has unique properties. Physical currency and cryptocurrency are fungible, which means that they can be traded or exchanged for one another.

- NFT stands for a non-fungible token, which means it can neither be replaced nor interchanged because it has unique properties.

Key Features of NFT -

- Digital Asset - NFT is a digital asset that represents Internet collectibles like art, music, and games with an authentic certificate created by blockchain technology that underlies Cryptocurrency.
- Unique - It cannot be forged or otherwise manipulated.

- Exchange - NFT exchanges take place with cryptocurrencies such as Bitcoin on specialist sites.

How Does NFT Work?

- The majority of NFTs reside on the Ethereum cryptocurrency's blockchain, a distributed public ledger that records transactions.
- NFTs are individual tokens with valuable information stored in them.
- Because they hold a value primarily set by the market and demand, they can be bought and sold just like other physical types of art.
- NFTs' unique data makes it easy to verify and validate their ownership and the transfer of tokens between owners.

What is NFT and How Does NFT Work? The Ultimate Guide
Lesson 17 of 31By Simplilearn
Last updated on Sep 15, 20222321603624
PreviousNext
Table of Contents
What is NFT?
How Does NFT Work?
Examples of NFT
What is NFT Used For?
Why Are NFTs Becoming Popular?
View More
Imagine buying a piece of digital artwork on the Internet at a reasonable price and getting a unique digital token known which proves your authority over the artwork you bought. Wouldn't it be great? Well, that opportunity exists now, thanks to NFTs.

NFTs are currently taking the digital art and collectables world by storm. Just as everyone worldwide believed Bitcoin was the digital answer to currency, NFTs are now pitched as the digital answer to collectibles. Asa result, digital artists are seeing their lives changing thanks to the massive sales to a new crypto audience.

If you are interested in NFTs and want to explore more about what they are, you have come to the right place. Let's dive in and see what all the fuss is about!

Professional Certificate Program in Blockchain

in Collaboration with IIT KanpurENROLL NOW

What is NFT?

NFT means non-fungible tokens (NFTs), which are generally created using the same type of programming used for cryptocurrencies. In simple terms these cryptographic assets are based on blockchain technology. They cannot be exchanged or traded equivalently like other cryptographic assets.

Like Bitcoin or Ethereum. The term NFT clearly represents it can neither be replaced nor interchanged because it has unique properties. Physical currency and cryptocurrency are fungible, which means that they can be traded or exchanged for one another.

NFT stands for a non-fungible token, which means it can neither be replaced nor interchanged because it has unique properties.

Key Features of NFT -

Digital Asset - NFT is a digital asset that represents Internet collectibles like art, music, and games with an authentic certificate created by blockchain technology that underlies Cryptocurrency.

Unique - It cannot be forged or otherwise manipulated.

Exchange - NFT exchanges take place with cryptocurrencies such as Bitcoin on specialist sites.

Read more: Best Cryptocurrencies for Long-term Investment in 2022

Blockchain Bootcamp

Master the architectural principles of Blockchain.ENROLL NOW

Cryptopunks is a notable example of an NFT. It enables you to buy, sell and store 10,000 collectibles with proof-of-ownership.

How Does NFT Work?

Now that you've taken your initial steps in understanding what an NFT is, you should continue on and learn about how an NFT works.

The majority of NFTs reside on the Ethereum cryptocurrency's blockchain, a distributed public ledger that records transactions.

NFTs are individual tokens with valuable information stored in them.

Because they hold a value primarily set by the market and demand, they can be bought and sold just like other physical types of art.

NFTs' unique data makes it easy to verify and validate their ownership and the transfer of tokens between owners.

Examples of NFT

The NFT world is relatively new to people. Here are some examples of NFTs that exist today:

- A Digital Collectible
- Domain Names
- Games
- Essays
- Sneakers in fashion line

What is NFT Used For?

People interested in Crypto-trading and people who like to collect artwork often use NFTs. Other than that, it has some other uses too like:

- **Digital Content** - The most significant use of NFTs today is in digital content. Content creators see their profits enhanced by NFTs, as they power a creator economy where creators have the ownership of their content over to the platforms they use to publicize it.

- **Investment and Collaterals** - Both NFT and DeFi (Decentralized Finance) share the same infrastructure. DeFi applications let you borrow money by using collateral. NFT and DeFi both work together to explore using NFTs as collateral instead.
- **Domain Names** - NFTs provide your domain with an easier-to-remember name. This works like a website domain name, making its IP address more memorable and valuable, usually based on length and relevance.
- **Gaming Items** - NFTs have garnered considerable interest from game developers. NFTs can provide a lot of benefits to the players. Normally, in an online game, you can buy items for your character, but that's as far as it goes. With NFTs, you can recoup your money by selling the items once you're finished with them.

Even celebrities like Snoop Dogg, Shawn Mendes, and Jack Dorsey are taking an interest in the NFT by releasing unique memories and artwork and selling them as securitized NFTs.

Why Are NFTs Becoming Popular?

NFTs have actually been around since 2015, but they are now experiencing a boost in popularity thanks to several factors. First, and perhaps most obviously, is the normalization and excitement of cryptocurrencies and the underlying blockchain frameworks. Beyond the technology itself is the combination of fandom, the economics of royalties, and the laws of scarcity. Consumers all want to get in on the opportunity to own unique digital content and potentially hold them as a type of investment.

When someone buys a non-fungible token, they gain ownership of the content, but it can still make its way over the Internet. In this way, an NFT can gain popularity — the more it's seen online, the more value it develops. When the asset is sold, the original creator gets a 10 percent cut, with the platform getting a small percentage and the current owner getting the rest of that revenue. Thus, there is potential for ongoing revenue from popular digital assets as they are bought and sold over time.

Authenticity is the name of the game with NFTs. Digital collectibles contain distinguishing information that make them distinct from any other NFT and easily verifiable, thanks to the blockchain. Creating and circulating fake collectibles doesn't work because each item can be traced back to the original creator or issuer. And, unlike cryptocurrencies, they can't be directly exchanged with one another (like baseball cards in real life) because no two are the same.

How is an NFT Different From Other Cryptocurrencies?

Although NFTs are created using the same kind of programming language as other cryptocurrencies, that's where the similarity ends.

Other Cryptocurrency

- Cryptocurrencies are "fungible"; they can be traded or exchanged for one another. They're also equal in value.
- For example, one Bitcoin is always equal to another Bitcoin, or one Dollar is always equal to one Dollar.

NFT

- Each NFT acts as a digital signature that makes it impossible for them to be exchanged for or equal to one another.
- For example, The Last Supper is a painting of a kind and cannot be exchanged with another painting.

How to Buy NFTs?

Having understood what NFTs are used for and its specific advantages over other cryptocurrencies, you might want to venture into buying NFTs. If so, you will need to acquire some essential items before you do it:

- You'll need a digital wallet that allows you to store your NFTs and cryptocurrencies.
- Then you need to purchase some cryptocurrency depending on what currencies your NFT provider accepts, most likely Ether. You can use platforms like OpenSea, Coinbase, Kraken, PayPal, etc., to buy cryptocurrencies.
- Once you've made your cryptocurrency purchase, you can move it from the exchange to your wallet.

Bear in mind, that many exchanges charge a small percentage of your crypto purchase transaction as fees.

Review of the Best NFT Marketplaces

NFT marketplaces serve as gateways to the NFT industry. Therefore, they are absolutely necessary if you are interested in buying or selling blockchain-based digital assets including art, music, or other assets. Think of NFT marketplaces as the anchor to the emerging NFT sector, responsible for facilitating the millions of dollars of trades executed daily. They can also be used to mint NFTs. Therefore, it is not a matter of whether or not you will ever need an NFT marketplace, but a question of which one you should opt for.

Choosing an NFT Marketplace

Before choosing an NFT marketplace, you must understand that they usually focus on a specific niche. This means you will find platforms that focus on digital art, in-game assets, or other niches. It is good to know what you are looking for before picking out an NFT marketplace. Another thing you need to consider is the number of users using the marketplace. It is vital to choose a marketplace that has a lot of people who are actively using it, as it would increase the liquidity and volume of NFT trades. Also, having more activity means you are likely to find competitive prices. Finally, you need to know the infrastructure, network and governance setup of the marketplace and how it impacts the way you access both the NFT market and your NFTs. This is something that might be difficult to determine if you are new to crypto. You need to find out if the marketplace is centralized or decentralized, which network is it running on etc.

Centralized marketplaces often operate as the middlemen between users and the NFT market, while decentralized options enable more direct access to the market. Also, centralized NFT marketplaces store NFTs on behalf of users. In contrast, decentralized alternatives let users have more control over their assets. Another thing you need to know is the blockchain network of the marketplace as well as payment options available to purchase NFTs. Last but not least, due diligence is a must, since there are plenty of scammers within the crypto space. Thus, it is vital to assess how safe your digital assets and personal information are on the platform, and what security measures the platform has in place to prevent fraud.

Let us go over a few top NFT marketplaces that exist in 2022

OpenSea

Currently, this protocol is considered the largest NFT marketplace in terms of volume. It was launched in 2017 with over 600,000 users and has processed over $10 billion worth of NFTs. Unlike most NFT marketplaces that exist today, OpenSea is quite easy to understand. You only need a few clicks to unlock NFT minting solutions and a vast NFT economy. Most importantly, it is a decentralized marketplace.

Rarible

Like OpenSea, Rarible runs a decentralized network and has taken a step further to introduce a community-focused governance system anchored by an ERC20 token called RARI. This protocol has processed over $270 million in NFTs so far. The team behind the protocol has managed to assemble the right tools for users to navigate the NFT marketplace. Also, the platform supports multiple blockchains such as Ethereum, Flow and Tezos, which allows users to mint, buy, and sell NFTs from other blockchains.

Nifty Gateway

There are not many NFT marketplaces out there that can boast the exclusivity offered by this protocol. The platform serves as a hub for buying and selling exclusive digital arts. The platform places great emphasis on authenticity and creativity, where only verified digital artists are allowed to mint and list NFTs on Nifty Gateway. This significantly reduces the chances of buying fake digital art on the platform.

SuperRare

This platform is considered a high-end variant of Rarible and OpenSea since it features digital arts vetted by the community before they can be listed on the website. This means the platform may be lacking in volume and trading activity when compared with the other alternatives. However, it makes up for it in its exclusivity. This makes the platform an ideal place to engage with an NFT community that understands the importance of authenticity and exclusiveness.

NBA Top Shot

This platform focuses on monetizing NBA short video basketball highlights or moments. These short clips are tokenized on the blockchain and sold to fans and collectors worldwide. Think of it as trading cards that exist on the blockchain. What makes this platform quite appealing to many users is that you can buy "moments" using fiat.

Mintable

This is an Ethereum based network that focuses on enabling easy-to-use services for NFTs across four categories, including art, videos, music and collectibles. The protocol allows creators to enjoy gas-free minting services. Also, it utilizes a decentralized governance system with its DAO anchored with an ERC721 token. By owning its NFTs, you get to have a say in its governance.

CHAPTER TWENTY-SIX

Comparing NFT, Cryptocurrency and Digital Currency

The world today is shifting from traditional wallets to digital wallets, a software-based program that secures user payment information. Digital currencies, as well as cryptocurrencies can be stored in digital wallets.

Digital currencies are electronic forms of currency coins and bills that can be stored in a digital wallet. Users can turn digital currency into cash by withdrawing it from a bank or an ATM. The encrypted form of digital currency is called cryptocurrency. This is where blockchain technology is applied, replacing financial institutions in validating transactions. There is also non-fungible token (i.e. NFT), a unique digital asset that represents real-world items. NFT is different from digital currencies and cryptocurrencies.

What is an NFT?

Non-fungible tokens are unique digital assets that represent real-world items, such as photos, music, videos and trading cards. They are managed in a digital ledger and are bought and sold online. For example, instead of purchasing an actual photo displayed on a wall, the buyer receives the original digital file. Almost any digital asset, such as a collectible digital character, virtual real estate, or an original post on social media, can be created and purchased as an NFT.

Non-fungible means that NFTs are not interchangeable. NFTs exist on a decentralized digital platform based on blockchain technology. Each NFT is different, which distinguishes it from fungible tokens that can be interchanged, such as cryptocurrencies. Specific values are attached to NFTs through certificates of authenticity to ensure that digital assets cannot be exchanged or replaced with each other.

Each transaction on the blockchain is written to a digital ledger that keeps public records to confirm the ownership of each item. Most NFTs exist on the blockchain of the Ether cryptocurrency. Like the Bitcoin blockchain, the Ethereum blockchain creates a permanent digital record of every transaction using the cryptocurrency. It also creates an undisputed ledger of all NFT transactions. The creator of the NFT retains the copyright to the project and has the right to copy it as many times as needed, while buyers still need the permission from the creator to make a copy. And each copy thus generated is also considered a unique NFT. NFT partners with auction houses and NFT marketplaces such as:

NBA Top Shot, an online marketplace running on the Flow blockchain where users can bid on, buy and sell digital highlights of NBA players. An NBA Top Shot video featuring LeBron James paying tribute to Kobe Bryant is sold for almost $400,000

OpenSea, a peer-to-peer marketplace for NFTs, virtual collectibles and rare digital items on the Ether blockchain.

Rarible, an open marketplace protected by the Ethereum blockchain that allows artists and creators to distribute and sell NFTs.

SuperRare, a digital art marketplace powered by the Ethereum blockchain. It's a platform where people can buy and sell NFTs from top artists.

Known Origin, an artist-driven platform running on the Ethereum blockchain where digital creators can validate, display and sell their collections and artworks.

Decentraland Marketplace, a decentralized virtual reality platform powered by the Ethereum blockchain. It provides a virtual space where users can create, experience and earn from the things they build and own.

Arkane Market, a marketplace of digital collectibles for general collectors and game players. Arkane Market is based on the Binance Smart Chain and the Ethereum and Polygon blockchains.

What is Cryptocurrency?

Cryptocurrency is a digital currency in cryptographic form that is independent from financial institutions in validating transactions. Cryptocurrencies are stored in digital wallets, a peer-to-peer system using blockchain technology to send and receive payments. When individuals transfer cryptocurrency, the transactions are recorded in a public ledger.

Some organizations have issued their own cryptocurrencies, or tokens, that allow people to trade for specific products or services offered by their companies. Individuals must exchange actual money for cryptocurrencies in order to make purchases. Here are some examples of popular cryptocurrencies:

Bitcoin, a cryptocurrency created in 2009. People can buy and sell bitcoins with other currencies on a marketplace known as a bitcoin exchange.

Ethereum, a blockchain-based software platform that enables developers to create smart contracts and distributed applications. The cryptocurrency of the Ethereum network is ether

Litecoin, an open source peer-to-peer cryptocurrency that allows people to make payments without going through banks or other third parties.

Tether, a stablecoin whose price is directly pegged to the value of the fiat currency it represents, such as the U.S. dollar, the euro or the Japanese yen. It is different from Bitcoin and ether, who have highly volatile prices.

What is Digital Currency ?

Digital currencies are electronic forms of monetary coins and notes that can be stored in digital wallets. Users can turn digital currency into cash by withdrawing it from a bank or an ATM. Although digital currency does not have a physical equivalent in the real world, it does have the same characteristics as traditional money. One digital currency can be acquired, transferred or exchanged into another digital one. A person can also use digital currency to pay for goods and services. Digital currency transactions can be sent to anywhere in the world.

A central bank digital currency (CBDC) is a centralized digital currency issued and regulated by the national central bank. CBDC uses digital tokens or electronic records to represent the electronic form of a nation's fiat. While there is not yet an officially launched central bank-backed digital currency, some central banks have initiated pilot programs and research projects to determine whether CBDCs are viable. The U.S. Federal Reserve Board is also exploring its own digital currency.

What are the differences among NFT, cryptocurrency and digital currency?

There are a number of differences among NFTs, cryptocurrencies and digital currencies. Unlike digital currencies and cryptocurrencies, NFTs cannot be traded or substituted for each other. Each NFT is different, distinguishing it from fungible tokens (such as digital currencies and cryptocurrencies) which can be traded or exchanged without loss of value.

Digital currencies are centralized, which means that the network of transactional states is regulated by a group of people and computers. On the other hand, cryptocurrencies and NFTs are decentralized, and belong to respective communities with set regulations.

Digital currencies are not transparent. For example, individuals cannot select a wallet address and view each of its transfers because the information is confidential. However, cryptocurrencies and NFTs are transparent. Any user can view any transaction made by another user since these are records placed in the public blockchain network.

Essentially, the digital currencies supported by central banks are electronic cash. Similar to cryptocurrencies like Bitcoin, CBDCs are data-based and do not exist in the real world. Unlike cryptocurrencies and NFTs, CBDCs are backed by the government, which means they are more likely to be adopted by individuals in purchasing goods and services in daily life.

CHAPTER TWENTY-SEVEN

STATE OF NFT DATA STORAGE

NFTs are tokens that represent the ownership of unique assets on a blockchain. Each NFT project has its own smart contract on the blockchain. The core of every NFT is its metadata, which consists of a description of the NFT such as the name, attributes, properties, etc., and a pointer to its media files (images, video, audio, etc.). Storing this information directly on a blockchain is expensive, so most NFT projects store their data elsewhere and only keep a link to it in their smart contract. Let us go over a few storage options available for NFTs.

Centralized Storage

Using a centralized server to store NFT data is the worst option of the few options available today. If the metadata and media files of an NFT project are stored on such a server, then the data will disappear forever if the creator stops maintaining that server, rendering the NFT 'blank'. Additionally, the person in control of the server can change the description and the content of the NFT at any point without the owner's permission. This completely defeats the purpose of NFTs. You do not have true ownership if your assets can be seized, altered, or censored. The only solution lies in using decentralized storage to prevent seizure, alteration, and censorship. The two most popular decentralized options for storing NFT data are the InterPlanetary File System (IPFS) and Arweave.

IPFS

IPFS is a peer-to-peer file storage network. An array of computers or nodes stores files uploaded to the network, and unique hashes are used to identify these files. The biggest difference between IPFS and web-based file storage is that IPFS uses a content-based address system. When a file request is made, the network finds a node that holds that file using its hash and serves it to the requestor. However, the weakness of IPFS is that persistency is not guaranteed. This means that data uploaded to IPFS will not remain there permanently. A file will only exist on IPFS as long as one of the network nodes stores the content and makes it available, also referred to as 'pinning' it.

When it comes to storing their files on IPFS long-term, most NFT projects and marketplaces either pin their data manually or use a pinning service to ensure that there is always at least one IPFS node that holds a copy. If the service maintaining an NFT's IPFS data was to fail and stop pinning files, all the stored information would be lost over time as nodes that held copies clear their memory caches or get shut down.

Arweave

This is a decentralized file storage network that guarantees persistency. Users pay a one-time fee to cover the cost of 200 years of storage. The 200-year benchmark is an extremely conservative estimate based on the decreasing price of physical data storage. If costs fall faster than estimated, Arweave files will be stored far beyond 200 years. Miners or computers in the Arweave network are incentivized using the $AR token to replicate and store copies of data that few other miners are storing. This ensures that files are not lost over time, with the need for ongoing maintenance by the original uploader. The protocol stores data in a structure known as blockweave. Each new data block is connected to the previous block and a historical one. Miners must prove they have access to these randomly chosen historical blocks to mine new blocks and earn rewards, which ensures that older blocks are preserved.

On-Chain

Using the two listed options above is much better than relying on centralized storage. However, it still requires pointing off-chain. Storing the NFT metadata and media on the same chain as the NFT is the most anti-fragile approach, but the cost of storing data on-chain is high. NFT projects that keep data on-chain utilize various compression techniques to lower this cost.

Breakdown of Adoption

Ethereum

IPFS is the most popular medium of NFT metadata storage on Ethereum. Currently, 48% of the top 100 trading NFT contracts by trading volume have their metadata stored on IPFS. Surprisingly, centralized serves are the second most popular option on the network.

Solana

On this network, Arweave reigns supreme when it comes to storing NFT data, with 90% of the top trading projects preserving their metadata here. The guarantee of persistence and lack of maintenance requirements makes Arweave an appealing option to projects in newer ecosystems where IPFS does not hold as much market share. Also, some of the most popular toolkits for minting Solana NFTs, such as Metaplex, uses Arweave as the default storage method.

Polygon

The NFT ecosystem on this blockchain has a high risk of centralization since 61% of the top trading projects rely on private servers for their metadata storage.

NFT USES IN THE METAVERSE

What are NFTs and the Metaverse?

If you want to understand the role of NFTs in the emerging metaverse, then you need to find the right answer to "What is NFT and metaverse?" before you move any further. NFTs or non-fungible tokens are a new class of digital assets, which are unique, indivisible, and immutable. They help in representing the ownership of digital and physical assets on the blockchain. Starting from digital artwork to the gaming industry, NFTs are making a huge impact everywhere.

In order to perceive the role of NFT in metaverse, you should know what the metaverse is. You can think of the metaverse as a digital environment running on the blockchain, where technologies such as VR and AR could serve as the visual component providers. The decentralized nature of the blockchain offers the prospects for unlimited business opportunities and social interaction. Metaverse offers extremely versatile, scalable, and interoperable digital environments. Most important of all, the metaverse blends innovative technologies with models of interaction between participants from individual and enterprise perspectives.

Is NFT Part of Metaverse?

Almost all discussions around the metaverse are pointing towards the possibilities of blending the metaverse and NFTs together. At the same time, many people also assume that NFTs are just another component in the broader metaverse. As a matter of fact, you can find that NFTs and metaverse are considered almost synonymous with each other.

The primary reason for such assumptions points towards sudden bursts of growth for NFTs in the field of blockchain gaming. It is reasonable to infer that the metaverse will shape up only through virtual worlds. Interoperable metaverse games can drive the development of the metaverse by serving the virtual worlds.

In addition, the association of real-life identities with digital avatars presents opportunities for defining access to the metaverse with NFTs. The first example of the metaverse NFT token was evident in 2019 with the instance of NFT-controlled access. The first NFT.NYC conference in 2019 used an NFT-based ticket for allowing entry to the event. Even if no one could call the conference the "metaverse," it definitely set a favorable precedent for the NFT metaverse interplay.

With a promising benchmark, many new projects have emerged in recent times for capitalizing on the intersection between NFTs and the metaverse. The projects are basically focusing on introducing massive transformations in the approaches for online interaction. The example of Decentraland shows how users can gain ownership of real estate in the metaverse with LAND tokens.

Will NFTs Build the Metaverse?

The metaverse is a massive concept, and NFTs can serve as a key concept in the broad ecosystem. NFT metaverse projects would drive the possibilities of using NFTs as deed to virtual property. NFTs could help in gaining exclusive access to enter the location in metaverse alongside allowing access to others.

Interestingly, the smart contract functionalities in the NFT could also help in selling real estate on the metaverse. The use cases of NFT in metaverse would focus primarily on NFT-controlled access in the initial stages of metaverse development. Just like the first-ever real-world example of implementing NFTs in the metaverse, NFT-controlled access could help in ensuring VIP access to real-life events and the events in metaverse.

NFTs could also serve a useful role in airdropping branded merchandise or special access privileges to followers. Apart from driving the efficiency of fan engagement, NFTs could introduce interoperability outside the metaverse with infrastructure supporting the features of location-based engagement and augmented reality. So, it is quite clear that the metaverse and NFTs are made for each other.

Effect of NFTs on Metaverse

In your quest for the answers to "Is NFT part of metaverse?" you might have found the different ways in which NFTs can help in building the metaverse. However, it is important to identify the significance of NFTs in changing the fundamental design of the metaverse. You must have noted that NFTs could introduce disruptions in the conventional social network precedents of user interaction, transaction, and socialization in the metaverse. So, how would these effects translate broadly onto the metaverse? Here are some of the highlights of how the metaverse NFT interplay would play out in the future.

- ### *The Road to a Fair and Transparent Economy*

As of now, individual users and enterprises could easily represent their real-world assets and solutions in a digital decentralized environment. The metaverse could open up to more real-world assets through the use of innovative gaming models in synchronization with interoperable blockchain games.

The role of NFT in metaverse would become more prominent with new models such as the play-to-earn gaming model. It not only offers the opportunity for using NFTs to drive engagement in the metaverse but also offers to empower chances to players. On top of it, play-to-earn games offer a fair gameplay experience by allowing complete ownership and control of assets to the players.

One could not help but notice the significance of play-to-earn gaming guilds in fuelling the growth of the NFT metaverse interplay. The guilds serve as intermediaries which purchase in-game NFT resources such as assets and lands. Then, they lend the assets and land to players who can use them in different virtual worlds for earning yields. In return, the play-to-earn guilds would only take a trivial share of the earnings. As a result, you can find the perfect basis for a fair and open economy in the metaverse by leveraging NFTs.

The guilds could lower the barrier to entry for play-to-earn games by offering the head start to players without upfront capital. Therefore, you can notice the possibility for a fair economy in the metaverse, which allows everyone to participate. Users could also trade their NFT assets like in-game collectibles and digital real estate on NFT marketplaces without any barriers.

The role of NFT in metaverse is clearly evident in the fact that blockchain offers transparency and immutability. The fair and open economy in the metaverse depends a lot on these properties. Now, the fundamental law of supply and demand would drive the scarcity of NFT and their on-chain value. As a result, you could not find any possibilities for artificial value inflation. So, you can see how the metaverse and NFTs work together to create a transparent and fair economy.

•

New Generation of Community, Social and Identity Experiences

The effect of NFT metaverse projects would also play a significant role in transforming the identity, social, and community experiences of users in the metaverse. Users could showcase their support for a specific project or express their opinions regarding the virtual and real worlds by holding NFT assets. As a result, like-minded NFT owners could form communities for sharing experiences and collaborating on content creation.

The trending example of NFT avatars shows how the metaverse NFT connection is transforming the world itself. NFT avatars are representatives of a player's actual self and the one they imagine. Players could use their NFT avatars in the form of access tokens for entering and switching between different locations in the metaverse. You can perceive NFTs as the extension of real-life identities of users with complete ownership, control, and flexibility for building virtual identities.

With NFT avatars, users could gain virtual membership to a wide range of experiences in the real world and metaverse. Therefore, the combination of metaverse and NFTs could improve the social and community experiences for users. The applications of NFT avatars in metaverse for startup launches and content creation also showcase their potential.

•

New Trends for Real Estate

Virtual worlds mean a lot of virtual space and real estate. You could use NFTs for gaining complete ownership of virtual spaces in the metaverse. With the help of the blockchain, users could easily prove ownership of the asset alongside developing virtual real estate.

One of the notable use cases of such NFT metaverse projects includes selling virtual land for profit. You can also rent land for passive income alongside developing various structures such as online shops or hosting events.

Decentraland is the most popular example for showcasing the digital real estate scenario in the metaverse. Recently, Decentraland conducted a virtual fashion exhibition, and that too in collaboration with Adidas. The exhibition showcased the auction of fashion designs as NFT. So, there is no hesitation in thinking about possibilities of auctions for virtual spaces in the metaverse in future. The popularity of virtual real estate has also attracted interest from music artists for exercising ownership over their work. Digital real estate would broadly refer to ownership of digital assets in the future, and every NFT holder would have a space in the metaverse.

NFT Uses In The Metaverse

Because NFTs are generally associated with websites and transactions that occur through web browsers, and because the metaverse is mostly VR-based, there might be some confusion about what their common ground is — and whether there is any in the first place. Thankfully, despite the relative novelty of both concepts, several companies have already found creative and fruitful ways to use both simultaneously.

1. Virtual marketplace. With apps like VRChat, spaces for communication in VR are already thriving, and it is not a huge leap to assume that these spaces can also serve as a fertile trading ground for NFTs. Sellers can easily provide links and previews to assets on the web or mint assets directly in the VR landscape.

VR and NFT marketplaces can appeal to many brands in various industries, and Nike is a good example. It's already dipping its toes into the metaverse with its own virtual "Nikeland" and has now acquired a studio (RTFKT) known for making NFTs of products. Perhaps it is only a matter of time before we see the two concepts meet in "Nikeworld."

2. Art gallery. VR is perhaps the best possible platform (short of an actual brick-and-mortar building) for viewing art. You get to see it up close with every detail and from every angle. This type of solution differs from a marketplace because the prices are already set (and not negotiated), the assets are all of one type (art compositions) and the atmosphere is much more relaxed.

For example, many museums are currently placing NFT artwork in metaverses such as Cryptovoxels, powered by the Ethereum blockchain. According to The Art Newspaper, Cryptovoxels hosts "art galleries and museums, including San Francisco Museum of Modern Art and the FC Francisco Carolinum Linz, Austria."

3. New frontiers. Real estate can be a pretty lucrative industry to work in in the physical world, and the same could apply to the metaverse. We are not referring to real homes being sold digitally but rather digital land and territories being partially or completely sold for further user development.

This case is more easily illustrated with an example. Decentraland is a virtual territory where plots of land can be sold as NFTs, and everything is represented in 3-D. This "country" has its own cryptocurrency and is slated to enter the metaverse (make the world accessible to VR users) later in 2022.

How To Implement A Metaverse With NFTs

As you may have noticed, the metaverse is still a pretty new concept, and only a handful of companies have already built real solutions in this field that implement NFTs. Thus, if you see a use case for the combination in your business and have the resources to make it happen, you could be one of the first companies in your industry to take advantage of these two trends.

Because most companies do not have any VR developers employed on their payroll full time, we might recommend looking to work with a company that has many years of experience in building immersive apps. Companies might consider going down this road even if they have a few local developers, as they might lack platform-specific knowledge of VR software such as building with Unity and Unreal or implementing movement tracking. Knowledge of blockchain and NFT minting will also be helpful unless you want to take on these technical aspects yourself.

Hopefully, now you know the main ideas behind the two concepts and have a sense of where the market is headed. If you choose to embrace the metaverse and NFTs in your business, it could be a great chance to break away from competitors and paint your business as a future-oriented one.

Final Words

The numerous potential associated with the NFT metaverse combination would transform the future. You can see how NFTs bring ownership and uniqueness while the metaverse gives a digital world where everything is possible. The combination of the digital world and a way to represent real and digital assets in the world would change the economy and social experiences. While many assume that NFTs are a part of the metaverse, and some think that NFTs are the building blocks of metaverse, it is clearly evident that NFTs and metaverse would open up a broad range of opportunities. Learn more about the metaverse and explore the possible ways for using NFTs in it.

Conclusion

Without a doubt, the Metaverse will have far-reaching consequences for our society. It will change how we communicate, advertise ourselves, and brand ourselves. Furthermore, this cutting-edge technology will bring new opportunities as well as challenges. The metaverse has the ability to unleash massive amounts of creativity while also broadening our economic, entertainment, and cultural horizons.